CHAKRAS

Also by Tori Hartman

Chakra Wisdom Oracle Cards: The Complete Spiritual
Toolkit for Transforming Your Life

Chakra Wisdom Oracle Toolkit: A 52-Week Journey
of Self-Discovery with the Lost Fables

How to Read the Cards for Yourself and Others
(Chakra Wisdom Oracle)

CHAKRAS

• • • •

USING THE CHAKRAS
FOR EMOTIONAL, PHYSICAL, AND
SPIRITUAL WELL-BEING

{ A Start Here Guide }

TORI HARTMAN

ST. MARTIN'S
ESSENTIALS

The information in this book is not intended to replace the advice of the reader's own physician or other medical professional. You should consult a medical professional in matters relating to health, especially if you have existing medical conditions, and before starting, stopping, or changing the dose of any medication you are taking. Individual readers are solely responsible for their own health care decisions. The author and the publisher do not accept responsibility for any adverse effects individuals may claim to experience, whether directly or indirectly, from the information contained in this book.

First published in the United States by St. Martin's Essentials,
an imprint of St. Martin's Publishing Group

www.stmartins.com

The Library of Congress Cataloging-in-Publication Data
is available upon request.

ISBN 978-1-250-21002-9 (trade paperback)
ISBN 978-1-250-23662-3 (ebook)

First Edition: November 2019

10 9 8 7 6 5 4 3 2 1

TO JOEL, GWEN, CHRIS, AND THOSE WHO SILENTLY OPEN THE
THE DOOR FOR MIRACLES

X
TORI

CONTENTS

NIGHTTIME RITUAL FOR CHAKRA HEALING   139

FINAL THOUGHTS   141

INTRODUCTION

Color energy has fascinated me for a long time. My work as a petite fashion model in the 1980s centered around color and books like *Color Me Beautiful*, which dictated to the world that you were a seasonal tone and was the new guide to buying clothing. Color itself was as loud as the decade, used as an accent and mixed in ways that made bold statements more brazen than the time period.

Even then I was intrigued with the messages in colors and how they made a statement. From the power tie, which was typically in a bold color, to the New York City "take me seriously" black wardrobe, color or lack of it set the trend for the decade. I didn't know it at the time, but my fashion book, *Fabulous You: Unlock Your Perfect Personal Style,* with its one chapter on what the color we wore meant, would be the beginning of my fascination with color and healing.

The stars aligned, and as things fell into place, I was guided to move to Los Angeles. A dream come true. No more winters—and more time to write, with my modeling days in the rearview mirror. I arrived in Los Angeles with enthusiasm, and shortly after my arrival, a series of angels began appearing and telling me stories in colors. I was angry and felt they were in the way of my writing the novel I would never write.

I had no idea at the time that those stories would be shoved in drawers and not find their way into my life for another ten years. And even then, I had no idea that they were the destiny I had asked for.

WHAT THE CHAKRA!?

The chakras were not on my mind until I began teaching. I later self-published the fables as an oracle card deck. They became so successful, I could no longer produce them on my own. I found the perfect publisher and the new name: Chakra Wisdom Oracle Cards. As of this writing, those Chakra Wisdom Oracle Cards have sold over 100,000 copies.

My research into the energy of color continued, and I began teaching how to read the cards by using the seven chakra system in an entirely intuitive way. While I had no formal training in the chakras, I recognized that the chakras themselves were the filters through which we could completely transform our lives. The more I worked with the chakras, the more I became aware of a power so misunderstood, I had no idea if I could translate it to those who had no idea of the power they themselves possessed.

The chakras contain everything we need to transform our

personal wounding, along with skills to effortlessly deal with life's challenges. The more I dove into the chakras, the more I uncovered a modern knowledge of the internal answers they contained—if we used them.

I witnessed breakthroughs right before my eyes by those who applied the simple chakra tools I had used for myself. People were transformed. I learned that our purpose is defined by our personal wounding and by what we try to ignore, and that our internal chakras hold keys to unlock the bliss we all seek.

The chakras are not a road but our map, which we all have, and one needs only to learn how to use it to find that elusive personal evolution and spiritual transformation we all crave.

BELIEFS ARE ALWAYS BASED ON FEAR, WHILE KNOWING IS FAITH-BASED

Years ago, when I arrived in Hollywood to embark upon my intuitive journey, I often socialized with actors and creative types. One day, while out with a group of friends, a well-known actor spun around on a barstool to face me.

"Do you really *believe* this crap that you do?"

I replied, "No. I don't believe it. I *know* it."

When I look back on that exchange, I had spoken in a definitive tone. Maybe this is why he simply had no comeback. There is no way to challenge that level of knowing. He never spoke another word to me. Ever.

This was another pivotal moment. People spend years trying to change beliefs, which is like rearranging deck chairs on the *Titanic*. Beliefs in and of themselves have an againstness energy, while knowing is faith-based.

For example, people who practice yoga don't *believe* they feel better, they *know* it. Thus, knowing is a true experience, while belief is a theory that may or may not apply to your life—yet many of us continue to carry this unnecessary weight.

ENLIGHTENMENT MADE SIMPLE . . .

. . . has been my saying for many years, so I tend to ditch the technical jargon. My goal is to bring your chakras to life and make them accessible to you. While I will cover some history, keep in mind that this book is a starting point to awaken and experience your chakras.

WHAT ARE THE CHAKRAS?

Chakra is a Sanskrit word that translates to "circle" or "wheel." The seven chakra centers in our body are "wheels" of energy in continuous motion. In our Western system the chakras correspond to the colors of the rainbow. The first chakra sits at the base of the spine and each one progresses inside the physical body up to the last one, which is located just above the head and is referred to as the crown chakra.

Each chakra vibrates at a particular frequency, and when combined with meditation practice, chakras are believed to be tools that align us with angelic realms. Each individual energy wheel has specific mind-body-spirit associations.

When you learn about these energy meridians (chakras) and how they operate, you more easily tune in with your own vibrational emotional, physical, and spiritual energy. What follows is a natural internal peace, along with an authentic harmony that few people truly enjoy in their lifetime.

These spinning energy centers contain a spiritual power to heal, rise above challenges, and activate the law of attraction.

Below is a brief overview of the seven chakras through our modern understanding of them. Each chakra has a Sanskrit name and a corresponding color.

> **CHAKRA TIP**
>
> Looking at chakra energy as an abstract idea, one may work with energy clearing. Yet working with it as an internal journey implies you have all you need inside of you.

THE CHAKRA

The First Chakra (Red): Muladhara

Located at the base of the spine, Muladhara is the root chakra. It is a grounding energy and represents a time of creation. Root healing is the beginning of personal individualism. It is associated with the color red, which ignites inner passion. Source is the chakra key.

The Second Chakra (Orange): Svadhishthana

Located in the abdominal area, this chakra governs circulation and motivation. It houses the womb and feminine energy, making it the catalyst for the movement of creation. Choosing and recognizing the difference between mature or immature emotions is the discipline of the second chakra. The color orange vibrates on this frequency. Sweetness is the chakra key.

The Third Chakra (Yellow): Manipura

Located in the solar plexus, the third chakra center is our instinct. When we get a "gut feeling," this is where we feel it. Hunches originate here, along with intuitive thinking and our fight or flight instinct. Radiant healing is meant to focus the thinking on higher consciousness. The color yellow vibrates with this chakra center. Radiance is the chakra key.

The Fourth Chakra (Green): Anahata

Here we journey above the physical and enter the domain of our heart. It is the part of us that opens us to give and receive love. It is a place of nurturing and care. Unstuck, unhurt, and unbeaten healing implies harmony and inspires an open heart. Green is the color that vibrates the fourth chakra center. Opening is the chakra key.

The Fifth Chakra (Blue): Vishuddha

This chakra vibrates in the throat area. This center rules our open and honest communication with others. Purity healing allows us to speak our truth. Since it rules expression of all kinds, you may notice that creative manifestation is at play. Blue vibrates the fifth chakra. Especially pure or truthful expression is the chakra key.

The Sixth Chakra (Indigo): Ajna

The sixth chakra, also known as the third eye, is the keeper of our inner truth. This is where we see into our past and the vast secrets of the inner knowledge. Intuition medicine is the mystical knowing wherein we will either see or deny what we know to be true. Associated with indigo, the power in this chakra is to see deep within. Insight is the chakra key.

The Seventh Chakra (Violet or Neutral): Sahasrara

This final chakra center is not located in the body, but above it. This is where the crown opens to the divine and allows inspiration to enter us. Crown healing is the connection to that which is infinite and unseen. The color violet and its vibrational energy resides in the seventh chakra. Infinity is the chakra key.

The Western Chakra

Our seven Western chakras rule key energy centers in our bodies. When connected with meditation, physical discipline, and intention, the chakras can create life-changing experiences.

Many people will tell you that chakras are as old as time. Indeed they are, yet there is not one direct link to define a direct connection back in history. Much of the historical timeline of the chakras today have overlapping concepts and long gaps in historical translation. Our Western chakra system has mixed and matched what was understood of its history, and in its development merged with color therapy, intuition, yoga, and the practice of manifesting what you desire, as in the law of attraction.

START HERE: CONCEPT ONE

There is no one true chakra expert or one definitive ideology. We are limited in our knowledge, in part due to the way in which our culture presents the chakras and its teaching to us. Rather than accept the chakras as a relatively new concept, great strides have been made to validate its power through attempts to prove an ancient connection. The chakras, however, cannot be traced by drawing a straight line back through time. This fragmented history does not diminish the power of the chakras in our lives today. Modern empiricism is real and has produced miraculous results for people. This is in essence what brought you to this point, where you have picked up this book; to learn more about you, and your inner map called the chakras.

THE COLOR THEORY THAT MADE 6 + 1 = 7

The carryover from the Eastern chakra systems, and there are many, that most closely resembles our current chakra system is the concept of $6 + 1$. This means that the first six chakras are within the physical body, and the seventh—the plus one—is outside the body.

This comes from the idea of three primary and secondary colors as the first six chakras. Since indigo is not a primary or secondary color, it was later added to accommodate the rainbow theory (our Western chakra theory), moving purple to the seventh chakra.

So if we look at the primary and secondary colors, as they translate into our Western system, it actually would then look like this:

- First chakra: red
- Second chakra: orange
- Third chakra: yellow
- Fourth chakra: green
- Fifth chakra: blue
- Sixth chakra: indigo
- Seventh chakra: violet or white light

The energy of indigo then is absorbed in our sixth sense or sixth chakra, which is in our own psychic or intuitive center. This makes our seventh chakra, which is the crown chakra just outside our body, the true universal consciousness, which vibrates the color violet or white light as a neutral tone, which stems from the idea that spirit is neutral.

In Summary

- *Chakra* is a Sanskrit word meaning "wheel."

- All but one chakra reside inside the body.

- Considered energy centers, each chakra vibrates at a different frequency and is associated with a different color.

- There is no true chakra expert.

- Western chakra evolution has occurred outside of historical connections to the past.

- Your chakras are an inner map. This is an intuitive and mystical path that you are here to discover.

Up Next: History

- Get ready! Some of the historical discoveries may not be what you hoped they would be.

- Many chakra books suffer from historical amnesia—when they're unsure, they use terminology to create a vague acceptance in the reader.

- Understand that most (if not all) of the chakra as we know it evolved from the practices (or beliefs, or studies) of intuitives, psychics, and monks.

- The counterculture of the late 1960s and early 1970s was a pivotal and vital component in creating a solid mind-body-spirit connection.

- Remember: YOU have chakras, and the focus of this book is YOU!

The most important thing to know about the chakras is how they affect you.

Experiencing your chakras is the key to learning what they are. Once you know what they feel like, further study will make sense to you.

HISTORY OF THE CHAKRAS

START HERE: HISTORY VERSUS SELECTIVE HISTORY

Many people who write about the chakras are referring to what they believe is an ancient map of seven beautiful rainbow colors. One of the most remarkable things about the seven chakras as we know them in the Western world is that there is an assumption that they can be traced from ancient history.

There is little, often scattered, information that has emerged about the chakras prior to the late 1800s, when ideas and practices were brought to the West via questionable translations from the Sanskrit texts which, when completed, were very difficult to comprehend.

I do believe that has as much to do with language and the way it is interpreted as it does to differing approaches to the chakra. Also, keep in mind that cultural lifestyles are as diverse as values. This may be a simple explanation as to the why—why the discovery and use of our chakras became so diverse.

One of the more readable books on chakra history emerged from Kurt Leland, a historian and researcher. In his book *Rainbow Body: A History of the Western Chakra System from Blavatsky to Brennan,* he dives deeply into the scattered early history and offers keen insight into our modern chakra evolution.

He writes:

I make a distinction between an indigenous "Eastern" chakra system that originated in India about a thousand years ago and a highly modified "Western" chakra system that developed from the former over a period of roughly a century, beginning around 1880—and that is now so divergent from its roots that it might as well have been invented without them.

It is important to note the way in which Leland describes the opposition of Eastern versus Western values to further comprehend the difference:

Eastern thinking prioritizes "inner states" over "outer action," whereas Western thinking does the opposite. Placed in relation to the chakra system, this distinction means the Eastern version is about passing through inwardly experienced states of consciousness, each more expansive than the last, until the ultimate "freedom"—liberation from the limitations of the self—has been achieved.

. . . However, the Western version is about developing the human potential for happiness in the outer world through actions taken in any of seven categories, ranging from the physical and emotional to intellectual and spiritual.

It becomes vital then to truly let go of the mythical "correct chakra history" and personal prejudice or judgment of it. To illustrate: I once read a review on a beginner chakra book that asked, "How can I even listen to this when it has nothing to do with the ancient teachings of the chakra?"

This comment glaringly reveals the arrogance associated with someone who thinks there are ancient teachings that are being ignored.

The truth is, the rainbow of seven chakras as we know it can be definitively traced to its humble beginnings in the 1970s.

The REAL Historical Evolution of the Western System

In the start of the decade that would be the 1970s, Esalen was a relatively new retreat center perched on the cliffs of Big Sur on the Northern California coastline and was home to the development of the human potential movement.

It was there that Roland Hunt's book, *The Seven Keys to Color Healing: Diagnosis and Treatment Using Color,* enjoyed a renewed interest.

In the same span of time, Ken Dychtwald's *BodyMind: A Synthesis of Eastern and Western Ways to Self-Awareness, Health, and Personal Growth* was published. It was during this era that the chakras became forever linked with the seven colors of the rainbow through this spiritual idea of color healing and meditation.

Ironically, it was an interview with Dychtwald in the August 1977 issue of *Yoga Journal* (coinciding with the publishing of his book) that brought this idea to a larger audience. Much of the chakra ideas of today developed from his and others' early work at Esalen that birthed and validated the merging of psychology and esotericism, which, at the time, chakras were considered to be.

The mind-body connection, meditation, and spiritual healing were all embraced at Esalen, and the Western chakra system of seven rainbow colors and healing points found a safe place to expand and become part of a landscape that would involve yoga, healing, chanting, meditation, Eastern theories such as Hindu and Buddhism, and Chinese medicine, which, over time, led to literally hundreds of theories on the chakras and where they began.

He Said, She Said

Terminology surrounding the chakra has a history in its own right. The *etheric body* relates to the human energy field or aura. While the term *etheric* is notably present in the early theosophical writings of Madame Blavatsky, it was only later formalized by C. W. Leadbeater and Annie Besant. Usage of the term became prominent (and necessary) when Hindu terminology was eliminated from the system of seven planes and bodies, or what we here refer to as the seven chakra.

Indigo, the color associated with the sixth chakra, is often a color attributed to the contemporary "new age" movement. In actuality, according to Kurt Leland's research it was Madame Blavatsky who first used the term "new age" when she brought some of these esoteric teachings to America.

Unfortunately some of her wisdom was dismissed, as her history included using séances to bilk people out of money. This is why I surmise that some historians use fluffy words to skip over our modern reinterpretation of chakras history—because much of it was developed by those in the esoteric arts. This gives rise to the skepticism around the use of chakras for many mainstream outlets.

Why Has This Not Been Common Knowledge Until Now?

If there is no one person or deity that left us the legacy of the chakras, one can be left with an empty feeling and think that none of it is real. Perhaps this is why no one has dared question it. Our chakras today are more of a modern development and an evolutionary idea than a historical tradition.

I surmise the reason many people create a vagueness around chakra history is the fear that if our present work is not directly connected to ancient teachings it invalidates it. Consider the image of Esalen as part of the hippie movement in the 1960s, and you will see why not one "chakra scholar" dared admit the awareness of our Western chakra occurred at an experiential retreat center like Esalen. Yet what better place would there have been?

Our modern chakra mysticism grew in a place that created a collaborative environment for people to experience and evolve using their intuitive wisdom.

Simplifying History

While it may appear that I have debunked ancient teaching, I am in actuality humanizing the evolutionary process of our own chakra wisdom. If this hypothesis is true, it validates the simple spiritual understanding that we have everything within us to *do all this and more.*

Before we go further, I'd like to give you a frame of reference for this information.

The Olympic Torch

The fire that signifies the opening of the Olympics is lit by a torch carried by not one, but many runners on the road to the games. Symbolically, the torch means *connecting the ancient games with the modern game*s.

The carrying of the torch is considered a great honor, as those who hold it carry the message of peace.

The opening of the Olympic games is represented by the

lighting of the final torch. No one person can take it all the way, rather a handoff occurs to keep the torch lit and ensure its journey is uninterrupted.

Can you remember the names of all those who carried an Olympic torch? Even if we don't remember each and every person, does that in any way diminish their contribution or the outcome?

Each handoff in the development of our modern chakra system has been like this. Each exchange was intended to bring the chakras as we know them closer to us, more relatable. More tangible.

Yet even the runner who lights the unified flame in the ultimate moment is soon forgotten, leaving you to step into the arena and discover for yourself the power of your own torch.

The chakras are your inner flames. They are powerful internal wisdom points, and the energy is handed off from one to the next. The relatively recent evolution of the seven chakra system in no way diminishes their importance in our life; it is rather a young tree with old roots.

This book is designed to validate our modern empiricism, which dictates that things are only true if we can experience them.

A VERY TEENY, BRIEF OVERVIEW OF CHAKRA HISTORY

To understand the disconnect of the chakra history, simply look at all of the differing languages, cultures, values, and spiritual beliefs involved. The vastly different places and people bring a multitude of ways to use the chakras as a spiritual journey.

Sanskrit Becomes a Western Fascination

Kundalini translates to mean "coiled." *Nadis* translates to "nerve endings," which are then believed to be coiled in our bodies like wheels. Sound familiar?

One of the ancient teachings is that each leaf of a lotus flower (in every chakra) had Sanskrit written on it that was a holy message.

The spiritual practice was to meditate on one Sanskrit character on each of the lotus leaves of a chakra until one by one they energetically disappeared from view. When every petal was cleared of the written word, the seeker was able to ascend to the next chakra. The petals of all the lotus leaves amount to the number 50, which is the exact number of letters in the Sanskrit alphabet. However, keep in mind that other cultures may differ on the number of petals and thus change this theory.

To give you a visual of this—in many books and charts, each chakra is a mandala that includes a lotus flower with differing amounts of petals on each.

The importance of obtaining or working with the chakras (energy points) in Eastern study was to transcend your human body and ultimately go through each of the chakra bodies to reach nirvana (releasing the heavenly body) in the final chakra.

Think of this discipline as akin to monks who spend their lives transcending their humanness to find their holiness.

So Someone Told You There Were More than Seven Chakras?

There are those who subscribe to the school of thought that there are thirteen chakras, or even hundreds. Many chakra teachers know of them, yet very few use them, as their presence is hidden to all but those who have transcended the seven and ascended to the higher elevations of skill and training.

In Eastern medicine the idea of many chakras stems from the healing practice of acupuncture, which works with nadis in the body; these nerve endings are referred to as nerve clusters.

The Chinese medicine use of chakra energy is concerned with where to find the most effective healing point and goes far beyond seven chakras. This is why we seldom work with these more advanced chakra clusters. In essence, being untrained and trying to work with these energies can create misalignment in our life-force energy.

Examining the elements of each culture reveals the very important answer in the underlying discussion of why no one really has the definitive count of the chakras, except the person experiencing them: only you can define your chakra energy and wisdom.

Whether it was the Chinese who developed it for medicine, Indian Buddhists and Hindus who tapped into the religious/spiritual (and yoga) practice, or the Westerners who developed their own ideas of harvesting magical results on the road to enlightenment, the seeds of the chakras belong to all of us.

One of the most enlightening concepts that comes from this awareness is that you have all of that ancient teaching already in you. The idea is to start here, and you can choose further historical study or personal study and application. Maybe both.

Summary

Remember: the most valuable takeaway from the study of chakras is YOUR connection with it. The gaps in history and the lack of true tangible connection led me to conclude that this study calls on us to use our intuitive side—we cannot understand an empirical study from a rational mind; it must rather be experienced.

You are going to experience our seven modern chakras here, and have one of the most powerful platforms to begin YOUR own evolutionary understanding and use of the chakras for yourself.

- The chakras have influences across vast cultures and times and cannot be traced to one definitive origin.

- The evolution of the chakras is a shared collaboration.

- The modern chakra system found its mainstream footing in the 1970s at Esalen.

- Our Western system does not comprise all ancient wisdom; it is rather a young tree with old roots.

- The relatively recent discovery of the Western chakra in no way diminishes its importance in our life.

WHAT TO EXPECT FROM THIS BOOK

- This is a starting point, not a definitive guide. The goal is to gain insight into your chakras and access their energies.

- The path to uncover your relationship with YOUR chakras is as unique as you are.

- Do not be intimidated by a lack of chakra knowledge. Think of this as a collage of you! What's more fun than that?

- This will bring you to a point where you can comfortably move to a deeper study if you choose.

- This is NOT a workbook, rather a FUN book. The activities within will combine *engagement* with a *little bit of explanation*. If you'll allow me to, I'll be your personal guide through the land of your own chakras.

- Working with chakra energy inspires, motivates, and opens up an entirely new way of looking at your world.

- Most important: You will gain the ability to change your life AND the lives of those around you.

INTRODUCTION TO THE
CHAKRA CHAPTERS

START HERE CONCEPT
In the most simplistic terms, this book is about our Western adaptation and use of the chakras from the Eastern Sanskrit.

The original idea of the Eastern, Hindu, and Buddhist ideals was to evolve from their human body, ascending spiritually one chakra at a time until they reached the seventh chakra of universal peace and oneness with the divine.

That ascension helps us understand the nirvana the Eastern traditions revered. The value of spiritual wisdom far outweighed any other personal need, want, or desire. They were set aside in favor of creating harmony within and a complete God consciousness.

Our Western society brought these ideas over as a way to create inner peace.

Unfortunately, the translated Sanskrit documents fell short of accuracy and left us with bits and pieces of scattered truths. As we filled in these truths, it became clear that most of the evolution of our Western interpretation was based on intuition and material channeled by various psychics and mystics.

I am in no way trying to invalidate the work we do today, quite the opposite. I am saying: let us trust our own selves. Our own evolution. Let us then work with what we know to be true and validate our own reality through our own instrument—our physical body, which does have chakras.

Let us remember that Madame Blavatsky coined the phrase "new age," and in many ways revolutionized the way we see the chakras today.

As you journey through each chakra, you will get a chance to experience your chakras and discover how to use YOUR energy centers as a map of inner guidance.

Let us remember that Joseph Campbell, whose work with archetypes and myths made him one of our early go-to philosophers, also had a hand in the evolution of our Western chakra.

The path of the chakras is one of emotional maturity and spiritual discipline; this personal recognition of bliss and the quest to attain it is what Campbell contributed with his hero's journey and other archetypes.

Let us remember that Carl Jung too was attracted to and worked with some of the Sanskrit ideas and was part of this passing of the torch!

You will notice as you travel through this book that many of Jung's ideas are woven into the text. This stems from the addition of psychological ideas for healing coming into the forefront during the human potential movement in the 1970s.

Why then would we not want to embrace our use of chakras?

One hypothesis I have come up with is that it is simply not validated by anyone; there is no concrete basis for the Western results of chakra practice. It stems from use and opinion, intuition and ideology.

Our society rarely validates the intuitive and esoteric experiences of the individual. Yet perhaps this is the exact thing that our Western development has intended all along.

What if . . .

Our interpretation of the chakras could stand alone? What if the connection to the past is not direct, that we modified some ancient ideas to use today? Is that okay? Is it still chakras as we know them?

I'm going to let YOU decide what works for YOU. I am going to share with you tools and techniques that I have used to experience my chakras. That is where we are going to start: with you.

Remember we are beginning with Western chakra, and remember: in the Western tradition we are much more focused on manifesting a peaceful existence than existing for a peaceful end.

Where we arrive is therefore not as important as our journey.

While the Eastern tradition is to evolve through the chakras to become free of the physical body, we in the West use our physical body to ascend into the life we desire.

In each chakra chapter, you will have an opportunity to see, feel, and experience the way the modern chakras can affect you in your daily routines. You will also find simple concepts to integrate into your life that will give you a way to experience the chakras as a living, breathing, transformational experience inside you. Think of your chakras as spiritual graduate school.

Each chakra has a survival (or lower) vibration and each one has a peaceful (higher) vibration, graduating you to the next chakra.

Start here with some basic ideas, through the lens of your inner wise self, and you will have a foundational understanding of your next steps.

In the individual chapters ahead, you will find ways to apply chakra traditions as well as some modern techniques to awaken your own spiritual awareness.

WHAT CHAKRAS ARE, AND WHAT THEY ARE NOT

- **What They Are:** Chakra "work" is a discipline of a spiritual practice whereby we transcend our human worries and discover peace and fulfillment.

- **What They Are Not:** Words and phrases that are in an ancient Sanskrit language that would change your life if only you knew what they meant.

- **What They Are:** Energy wheels inside you that comprise your soul's vibration.

- **What They Are Not:** The chakras are not accessed by understanding them. They are accessed by understanding ourselves.

And now, the Chakras ...

THE FIRST CHAKRA (RED): MULADHARA

Lotus: 4 petals. It is believed that the leaves of the lotus in the first six chakras add up to 50, one for each letter in the Sanskrit alphabet. In the early practice, the idea was to sound out each letter. As you meditated on it, when the letter disappeared, the energy would rise to the next chakra. The seventh chakra represents infinity with its thousand petals, as God consciousness never ends.

Governance: reproductive glands, hormones

Organs: reproductive organs

Meaning: root

Key Concept: family beliefs

Western Translation: foundation

Western Color Therapy: courage

Kundalini Aspect: *the raising of consciousness.* The first chakra is akin to the sleeping cobra—a life force energy that rests at the base of the spine.

Herbs and Spices: *cloves and cayenne pepper.* All spices and herbs that are associated with the first chakra are going to be noticed! Cloves and cayenne pepper awaken the taste buds and energize our first chakra. When used in homeopathic remedies they address the challenges of the first chakra.

First Chakra Physical Challenges

These include impotence, colitis, overeating, anorexia, and prostate issues. Challenges in the first chakra show up emotionally as:

- a desire to disappear (anorexia)
- family beliefs that shut down your own knowing
- compulsive eating (this masks being ungrounded)

Calming the First Chakra Physical Challenges

One of the first things to recognize is that family beliefs may be the cause of feeling ungrounded. Trying to change a belief and replace it with another is akin to replacing one fear with another. To shift this energy, ask yourself:

- What beliefs (fear-based thoughts) did my family teach in an attempt to keep me safe?
- What do I KNOW (your highest internal wisdom) to be true here?
- What new foundational energy (first chakra can represent old family beliefs) must I source my life from to do this?

Tip: If you feel lost or confused, that's okay. Finish reading this chapter, and then look at pages 124–126 on centering and chakra sound. You can return to this later. Breathe.

First Chakra Personal Challenges

Many issues that arise in this first chakra zone are often related to what is hidden, family restrictions, and what we don't admit.

Calming the First Chakra Personal Challenges

Personal instability is often created by beliefs. Rather than "change," replace, or erase a belief, it is more fun to expand your root base! Do the first chakra meditation later in this chapter since once you know how to shift spiritually, old family ideas can be set aside for your own internal knowing.

What is revealed can be healed.

THE FIRST CHAKRA BLOCKED

Many scholars and "gurus" like to discuss blocked chakras. What is interpreted as a block may actually be an indication that the chakra is *busy trying to heal*, and is sending you a message.

The first chakra is referred to as the seat of the soul and houses our hidden beliefs that we brought into this life. Think of it as what was needed for survival and inherited from our ancestors. However, if we imagine a coiled cobra, which is often the image held for the first chakra, we can ask ourselves: Will we awaken that cobra and unearth what is hidden? Or will we ignore what is a hidden part of our soul?

Most of us only have a vague sense of the beliefs that run our lives.

If this first chakra holds the energy of procreation, the Westernized idea of the chakras will bring inherited beliefs that are carried in our DNA. The modern chakras form a map that makes the energy accessible to us in tangible ways, allowing us to see and tap into the true power we have had all along.

CRYSTALS AND STONES OF THE FIRST CHAKRA

Crystals and stones are frequently used to open, cleanse, balance, activate, and heal the root chakra.

- **Red carnelian:** This is a light red semiprecious stone worn to attract strength and courage, creating a firm base to stand on.

- **Garnet:** This deep red semiprecious stone is used in meditation and body healing sessions.

- **Red jasper:** This earthy red semiprecious stone is a protection stone, creating a barrier between you and negativity.

- **Bloodstone:** Dark green with red spots, this semiprecious stone is worn as a barrier to outside influences and to foster self-esteem.

- **Smoky quartz:** This black crystal is used in meditation and law of attraction rituals.

- **Black tourmaline:** This black semiprecious stone is effective in spiritual grounding and solidifying your platform.

- **Obsidian:** This black organic stone is the opening of the root chakra and prophecy. It will support you in clearing old beliefs.

CHAKRA COLOR: RED

- **Attributes:** vital, sexual, passionate, energized, forceful
- **Statement:** I am self-motivated from the center of my being.
- **Impression:** passion

The color red illuminates what the first chakra represents. There are dozens of shades and hues assigned to the primary color of red. That means our eyes will focus on and take in the energy before we even assign a meaning to it. Lasers used for healing are red waves of energy, and we intuitively assign this healing to the invisible energy of red.

Tip: Color awareness is one of the simple ways to understand your chakras because we see color all around us, and our personal likes and dislikes prove that out. The more you apply color knowledge, the more accessible the chakras become.

Consider this: It is far easier to imagine the color red than to imagine your first chakra.

EVOLUTION OF MEANING

Common feelings in the first chakra are of being stuck, not being grounded, and not having what it takes to build and create what we came here to do. This chakra is often the one that will represent what has eluded you in this lifetime so far.

MODERN INTERPRETATION

We must look at our personal source. Where are our roots touching? What do we need to sustain what we are building? Next is an example of two roots and the route of each.

THE ROOT STORY

A number of years ago, after buying my first home in Los Angeles, I planted two apple trees in my yard. They were both six feet tall when planted, and each had an equal amount of sun and were well positioned to grow.

I researched what fruit trees needed to grow, and to my surprise, the roots of an apple tree need anywhere from 500 to 1,500 chill hours. That means a winter climate is what helps apples grow large because the ground needs to be cold for the root to be stimulated for fruit production.

Now in Southern California, if we get 200 hours of ground freeze it's nothing short of a miracle. So to trick the tree roots I tried an experiment. During the weeks from mid-October through mid-January, I put one twenty-pound bag of ice at the base of one of the trees for a week at a time.

The results were nothing short of extraordinary. In the first year the tree with the ice doubled in size and produced perhaps a half dozen apples. The other tree did not grow and produced two scrawny apples that ultimately fell off and died.

Year after year, I would ice the tree less and less, yet it still grew to be over thirty feet in size and produced more than a few dozen good-sized apples. The other tree stayed the same.

This story illustrates how profound it is to pay attention to our roots.

In the following meditation, I am going to invite you to experience your roots to demonstrate the power you hold within to energetically grow as wide and tall as you choose.

MEDITATION

I invite you to step into a waking consciousness meditation. That means you can read this meditation, and it will work. Notice and become aware that you are going inside, into the deepest part of you.

And as you breathe, become aware that by simply being *told* that the intention is to experience your roots, you are already in the energetic state of connection with your roots.

Breathe.

As you drop your shoulders I'm going to invite you to sink into your body.

Allow your eyes to loosely follow the words on the page.

As you do this, go ahead and plant your feet firmly on the ground.

Breathe.

Once again, drop your shoulders as you exhale and send anything out of your body that is not necessary to this moment.

If a thought takes you away, allow yourself permission to see it as a cloud in the sky and allow it to float away and then come back.

Shift your focus to the bottoms of your feet until you feel tingling on the bottoms of your feet.

These energies are your internal energetic roots, and they are connecting you to the pulse of the earth—allow them to energetically grow.

In your mind's eye, begin to see your energetic roots finding their natural space in the earth.

Breathe.

Drop your shoulders.

Simply observe where your roots are in this moment.

Do nothing—simply observe.

As you take a slow, deep breath, I'd like you to become aware of your roots, slightly stuck and struggling; perhaps there's a rock hindering one of them, or the soil is dense like clay.

Breathe and keep reading:

You can give your growing roots whatever they need. Is there an underground spring? This clean mineral water brings nourishment to your roots. Your roots are now growing beyond your current frame of reference.

Like the roots of a rose, which are strong enough to break through clay soil and thrive, I am going to now invite you to allow your roots to energetically grow stronger and wider—

Going deeper . . . And deeper . . . Into the earth.

And as they do this, I want you to begin to notice that these energetic tendrils are tapping into . . .

Beautiful rich soil . . .

Deliciously clean spring water . . .

Moist warm earth . . .

And these roots are now growing stronger and wider than you ever imagined.

Where you are growing is creating a new foundation.

Breathe in, coming to your waking consciousness; allow the energy from those roots to come straight up into you; and as it hits your first chakra at the base of your body, become aware of the internal strength that you have just created.

When you are ready, come forward, aware of this new energy—open your journal and take a few minutes to note the personal power you experienced within.

Welcome to the power, energy, and strength of the new foundation you have just established in your life. Welcome to the first stop on your chakra map.

CHAKRA EXERCISES

Journaling Time

Set the timer for 10 minutes. Sit quietly and allow yourself the time to experience your new foundation. If you choose not to write, give yourself this time to breathe and be at peace.

Contemplation

What will I do with my awakened personal power?

What would I like to start, create, or renew?

A RED FIRST CHAKRA CONCEPT

If our beliefs come from our family of origin, are they truly ours?

Yes and no. For example, a family member's depression may belong to them, and while you may have embodied the experience of sadness, it does not necessarily mean that you too are depressed. And, what if it does belong to someone else?

When we experience something, it becomes real and known by us. When we try to change a belief, we give up our own ability to create our own destiny.

When you stretched deeper and wider in the meditation above, you experienced a knowing of your own energy. You didn't have to believe in that experience, did you?

BELIEFS WILL STOP US IN THE FIRST CHAKRA

In the first chakra, it is important to look at that which empowers you and that which disempowers you. This energy represents your springboard, the very foundation on which you build your life. If you are building your life in an againstness energy, you will always find yourself in a weakened position. And consequently first chakra issues, illness, and instability will plague you.

Ironically, personal empowerment can sometimes come from acknowledging that a negative family projection may be true about you. When you acknowledge that you are fulfilling a belief about you, it becomes owned by you and therefore can be released by you.

> *When we build our foundation around a handicap we don't actually have, it can be disruptive, even earth-shattering.*

This chakra is where the energy of wasted time, and the sadness surrounding it, lives and is the best place to shore up a weak foundation.

> *Remember: Beliefs are always fear-based, while knowing is faith-based.*

APPLYING THE FIRST CHAKRA:
YOUR MAP HAS YOUR ANSWERS

Your root chakra is your inner map and the blueprint of your foundational energy. This treasure map will contain all the necessary elements for you to sustain what you choose to create.

FIRST CHAKRA DISCIPLINE:
HOW WE RELATE TO THE ISSUE IS THE ISSUE

A young woman was told by her parents that she'd been rejected from medical school. Fifteen years later, she found out that they had lied to her and that she had in fact been accepted. Her parents' lie had been to "protect" her. Why? Because both of them had washed out of medical school.

After she exploded emotionally (second chakra), she looked back at the first chakra and recognized that her family beliefs were not hers. They had been projected onto her. Once she

identified this, she was able to shed them. At the age
seven, she chose to give up the career she had settled
began medical school.

This is a powerful example of recognizing that we all have the
ability to no longer live under limiting beliefs that we inherited.

CHAKRA EXERCISE

Write About It

Tap into Your First Chakra Anytime / 30 minutes

Using the keywords and key phrases below, write out your story,
from where you were with family beliefs to where you are now
and to where you ultimately see yourself.

Be creative! Write your letter to your higher self and see how
many old ideas you can change into empowering ones!

Oh, and **HAVE FUN!!!!**

This is your personal rewritten first chakra story!

Keywords and Phrases That Relate to the First Chakra

- **Keywords:** foundation, base, grounding, platform, origins,
  beliefs, DNA, secrets, family, unsettled, unfocused, guilt,
  anxiety, resentment, suppression, depression, stuck, growth,
  anemia

- **Key Phrases:** changing the story of our past, family expectations of you, what we base our opinions on, no daughter/
  son of mine would ever do that, don't have a leg to stand
  on, having your feet planted firmly on the ground, having a
  right to be here, derivative value based on where you come
  from, fear of personal independence, family secrets, being
  held back

MANIFESTING INTENTION

Red stirs issues of creation to the surface. It is where we begin; where we propagate. A clearing begins here of all that stands in the way to our heart's desire. This is where you start your path, and your base of operations takes form. The beginning!

Now, if you could create ANYthing, what would it be? (Fill in the blank)

1. My deepest hidden desire is _____.

2. If my source energy is _____, then my outcome is _____.

3. What support do I need? _____.

Use your root meditation if need be. Do you need to go deeper? Was there more to uncover? What would you like your roots to drink or source from?

How prepared are you to face discarding old beliefs that no longer serve you?

WHEN YOUR FIRST CHAKRA IS UNSETTLED, LOOK TO THE PRIOR ONE

For all that manifests into physical form in the first chakra, the seeds of the idea are drawn from the universal consciousness in the seventh chakra.

If there is an energy disturbance in the first chakra, that means the root of the problem will be found in the previous chakra on the wheel.

For example, in the seventh chakra we are looking at universal concepts or ideas. If my seventh chakra universal idea is that the contribution I want to make is to write a book to heal the planet, and I'm not specific enough in the foundation I create in my first chakra, I may find that I don't have a solid enough grounding in the *idea* to make it physically happen.

First Chakra Reminder

Think of the seventh chakra as the place where we get seeds. They must be planted in the first chakra to take root. This is what a true foundation is, and what happens when an idea or person is grounded. Only then can things grow.

First Chakra Key Ideas

- Our foundation is based on beliefs that we carry with us, often inherited from our family of origin.

- We recognize that we must uncover our own truth.

- We can never rid ourselves of what is necessary for our journey.

- How we relate to the issue IS the issue.

- We recognize that an insecurity or fear may belong to a family member and is not necessarily ours.

- Self-realization does not mean leaving people behind, it means no longer carrying their beliefs as our own.

- The first chakra reveals to us that in growing our own roots deeper and wider we can create the foundation for our own life.

- Question if the beliefs you have are really supporting you.

LOOKING AHEAD

In the next chapter, we will look at the second chakra and see how our emotional life is directly tied to the meaning we have made of our life experiences in the first chakra. Your emotional maturity or immaturity is going to dictate the choices you will make and the path you will follow.

THE SECOND CHAKRA (ORANGE): SVADHISHTHANA

Lotus: 6 petals

Governance: sacrum, adrenal glands, the immune system and metabolism, fertility issues

Organs: Adrenal glands

Meaning: sweetness

Key Concept: pleasure

Western Translation: feelings

Western Color Therapy: emotional issues

Kundalini Aspect: The awakened cobra offers the opportunity for our greatest emotional fears, or emotions we try to avoid, to surface. The yogis' second chakra practice included transcending emotional pain—through guiding and directing their sexual energy. This is where the idea of kundalini comes into play in making these powerful energies usable in our everyday life.

Herbs and Spices: *turmeric.* Turmeric is believed to be an anti-inflammatory agent.

Second Chakra Physical Challenge

These include gallstones, kidney infections, prostate inflammation, bladder infections, and fertility issues. Challenges in the second chakra are highly charged as emotions are activated here. They frequently may be traced to:

- money fears
- feeling undervalued
- suppressed emotions (hiding our true feelings)

Calming the Second Chakra Physical Challenges

Since our emotions are filtered through our second chakra, they must be revealed in order to be healed. Imagine driving a car with one foot on the gas and the other on the brake. This is how your body experiences conflicting emotions.

Try using the centering and sound tools on pages 124–126 to concentrate on centering. Once you find your own center, write a love letter to the highly charged emotions above.

For example:

Dear Money Fears,

Here's why I love you . . .

Write until you feel complete. Do not force a solution. Try not to fix it. Just write the truth as you see it. Stay in your feelings.

Tip: You can use this technique for ANY physical issue; simply remember that it is being guided through your second chakra and is an emotional journey, not a cerebral one.

To Spot Dangerous Emotional States Here Are a Few Things to Look For

- extreme emotions—those which drive you to imagine or plan harmful actions

- indifference—simply wanting to deal with external symptoms and shutting down

- any emotional desperation that you simply cannot process and is not going away

Note: Please remember extreme emotional states can be dangerous. I encourage you to reach out for professional support. While it's hard to know if that's your situation, if these emotional states resonate for you, there is much to be gained from speaking to a professional and giving yourself the gift of support.

Second Chakra Personal Challenges

The biggest challenge in the second chakra is the meaning we make of an experience in any given moment. Emotional upset occurs when we can't see or understand how to move through blocks or problems. This creates a feeling of helplessness and leads to our responding with immature versus mature emotions.

Calming the Second Chakra Personal Challenges

You have an internal ability to empower yourself with mature emotional energy in any circumstance. As you move through this chapter, you will gain tools that open the door to clear thinking.

We never consciously choose emotional upset; it comes from the two greatest fears: that of losing what we have and of not getting what we want.

CRYSTALS AND STONES OF THE SECOND CHAKRA

Crystals that open, activate, and soothe the second chakra include:

- **Orange calcite:** A stone with physical and emotional restorative properties, it is associated with distance healing.

- **Moonstone:** This stone is a healer of hurt feelings; it allows self-soothing and emotional compassion.

- **Citrine:** The stone of self-improvement, it supports emotional clarity and clear thinking.

- **Orange carnelian:** This emotionally stabilizing stone allows fluid motion in the body, supporting dance and creativity.

- **Orange aventurine:** The stone of life force and emotional power, it brings confidence.

- **Amber:** This gemstone is fossilized tree resin. Used for those suffering from depression, it is a wonderful stone to journal with when working through challenging feelings. It draws love and joy into your life.

CHAKRA COLOR: ORANGE

The color orange and its emotional nature are assigned to the second chakra.

- **Attributes:** active, motivating, optimistic, courageous, sociable, enthusiastic, affectionate, humanitarian

- **Statement:** I can use my feelings to focus on my deepest desires.

- **Impression:** emotion

It is much easier to feel into the color orange than to imagine your second chakra.

EVOLUTION OF MEANING

At one time, chakra practice was a discipline; comfort and personal feelings were most likely not of vital importance to the original Eastern practitioners.

Western tradition seeks out positive emotions and stresses the value of feeling good. Concern about feeling good is a very westernized idea.

MODERN INTERPRETATION

In the more modern interpretation of the second chakra, the law of attraction equates emotion to manifesting.

When other people draw us into a lower emotional vibration, it is directly related to an immature feeling. When we try to "overcome" or "get over" something, it keeps us in a pattern of trying to deaden our feelings as a way of disconnecting from unresolved feelings.

Therefore in the second chakra, we learn that we never really overcome anything, we rather integrate it into the map of our life.

Let's look at the contrast between immature emotions, which simply have not evolved, and mature emotions, which are true freedom.

THE SACRAL STORY

In a class on multigenerational healing, a student named Molly stated that she was never going to forgive her parents.

I jokingly said that the forgiveness class was down the hall; she didn't have to forgive: that was not what this class was about. The class assignment was to find out as much as she could about her grandparents.

She insisted upon telling us why she was not going to forgive her parents. She revealed that she and her brother were raised in a cult. Her parents kept them prisoner for the first eighteen years of her life. She had never met her grandparents, so she really didn't know anything about them and had no interest in them at all.

I encouraged her to play along; after all, she signed up for a class that required it. She agreed.

Two weeks later she came in rather shaken, her face puffy from crying. She shared with us what she had just discovered:

One of her grandparents had spent his entire fortune in court fighting to get custody of her and her brother. He lost appeal after appeal until there was no more money. By then she had aged out of the courts and was on her own.

She had never met this grandfather, yet she discovered that on the day she registered for the class, he died.

I asked her how she felt about her parents now.

With her eyes off in the distance, she shared that it no longer mattered. The emotional upset that had once been there was gone. She no longer felt the massive anger or resentment she had carried with her throughout childhood.

Someone, somewhere, had profoundly loved her. A man she never met had spent everything he had trying to save her. The love he had for her both validated all the painful feelings and wiped them away in this awareness. She experienced love for the first time in her life.

This is the potential of our second chakra: emotional evolution that lifts us into our maturity.

CHAKRA EXERCISE

A Journaling Meditation / 17 Minutes

"The weak can never forgive. Forgiveness is the attribute of the strong."

—Mahatma Gandhi

Since every chakra has its own essence, you will notice that each activity, exercise, meditation, and even visualization in each chapter is going to take on the qualities of that chakra.

We can now imagine how the yogis felt as they spent hours upon hours in meditative discipline; moving toward the God consciousness as they evolved from the orange chakra, giving over their emotional life to the creator.

In the second chakra, in order to experience the depth of being profoundly loved, the first step is a meditative practice of self-forgiveness. It is important to note that we never really forgive others; rather we forgive ourselves for having judged them.

I'm going to invite you to breathe deeply, and with your eyes open as you read this, we are going to do a waking meditation—with a pen and a piece of paper. If you have one, pull out your journal and open to a fresh page.

On your piece of paper, draw a symbol or doodle at the top. This is your letterhead, and this next stop is your second chakra location on your internal map.

In just a moment, I'm going to invite you to write emotionally free-form. And here's how it occurs:

Breathe and step into your emotional body. Really experience and allow yourself to become aware of the feelings you are having right now. Now breathe and drop your shoulders, letting go of that awareness, and instead imagine that you are transported to a magical location in which you are going to write a letter from your yet-to-be-born self to the person you are now.

The unborn version of you in heaven is very much aware of your emotional life. I'd like you to imagine that you are now your unborn self—look only to the paper in front of you with pen in hand. They are all that matters in this existence. The only thing you are going to need to tell your future self in human form is describing the challenging feelings they will have in their life.

You are going to write this letter, beginning with Dear _____,

Then start to write!

This is going to be from the you that is unborn to the you that now exists. Make sure that you use the pronoun of you, not I, for you are writing to the future you a letter letting you know about your own emotional nature in human form.

When you are ready, set your timer for 17 minutes. Allow yourself to bring down white light from the heavens and sit quietly with the in-between times. Remember you have a lot to say.

Write this in free-form, in any way and manner you choose.

The most important takeaway is that you write until you are finished, or until your 17 minutes are done.

When your written meditation is complete, put it away for a twenty-four-hour period. This will allow you to read what you have written with a mature distance.

Giving yourself the space to mourn the loss of what was not given to you, as well as the time wasted in anger and expectation, is an important piece of self-forgiveness.

"The privilege of a lifetime is being who you are."

—Joseph Campbell

APPLYING THE SECOND CHAKRA: YOUR MAP, YOUR PATH

This next stop on your map is going to dictate the road you will travel.

Ready?

What feeling do you MOST want to avoid?

That feeling is currently dictating your life choices.

A SECOND CHAKRA TIP

In most cases, feelings people avoid are going to influence the decisions they make in their lives.

WHEN YOUR SECOND CHAKRA IS UNSETTLED, LOOK TO THE PRIOR ONE

Look back to the first chakra meditation. Remember growing your roots?

Where do you need to grow your roots to become more grounded emotionally? Refusal to take responsibility for our emotions (maybe from not wanting to let an abusive parent off the hook) is often a resulting pattern from a parent who lived in an immature space.

That does not mean you have to stay in that space.

Our Answers Are Already Inside

If you wish to raise your emotional vibration to the highest calling of the second chakra, it becomes necessary to separate your emotional life from the belief systems of your family of origin. *Or the meaning we have made of the experiences from our family of origin.*

When we live our life in a reactionary mode, it is the lower vibration that is running us, and it's very challenging to actually manifest any happiness.

This means that where the law of attraction is concerned, an immature second chakra will dictate an outcome that may be leading you into repetitive emotional disappointment.

> **A SECOND CHAKRA INSIGHT**
> Are our feelings controlling us, or are we harnessing their energy to guide us?

VISUALIZE IT—TAP INTO YOUR SECOND CHAKRA ANYTIME

Emotions run the gamut from feeling nothing to feelings so powerful they can drive us to extremes. This visualization is designed to give you a tool to see where you are at any time, and gain emotional perspective—on any situation in your life.

One of the easiest ways to do this is through our intuitive response to color.

Take a moment to visualize a rainbow of orange color tones.

Begin with a faint hint of orange through to a true orange, and as we saturate it more into deeper tones, finally the deepest orange you can imagine.

Take a moment to energetically step back and observe this fan of color in front of you.

Notice how the lighter colors stir less emotion than the darker colors.

Go inside for a moment and imagine your second chakra, two inches below your navel. Are you able to observe your feeling?

Look at the orange rainbow in front of you. Where do you sit on this span of color?

What color resonates with you?

Without reading further just yet, in your mind's eye, match your internal feeling to the visualized intensity of color tone.

The lighter the hue, the less intense the emotion in the moment. Be aware that when you go past the middle section into deeper tones, it may be helpful to use the meditative journal technique you learned earlier.

If you're just starting out on a new venture in your life, you may visualize a lighter color, as you have not yet discovered how you feel.

When you start here with visualizing all the shades of orange, you will begin to experience the vibrational power of the second chakra.

IDENTIFY AND PUT A NAME TO YOUR FEELING

The Antonym Approach

When we feel stuck, it can sometimes be challenging to identify the feeling we are having in the moment. On the next page are a sampling of keywords and phrases that relate to the second chakra. Look for the keyword that most closely describes your current feeling. If it does not fit, or you feel confused, go look up the antonym.

Keywords and Phrases That Relate to the Second Chakra

- **Keywords:** emotion, mature, immature, amusement, the unconventional, extroverts, fun, energy, activity, taste and aroma, feeling, pleasure, sensuality, intimacy, wellness, happiness, wealth, pleasure

- **Key Phrases:** What will I create?, withholding feelings, question the meaning you have made of your emotions, intimacy is IN-TO-ME-SEE, it is not something we get from others, it is who we are

MANIFESTING INTENTION

Here is where the rubber meets the road. You have begun the journey into using your feelings to guide and empower you in personal manifestation. Action and movement prevail. You will soon walk the path you have previously only talked about.

Second Chakra Key Ideas

- We begin by asking ourselves: How do I feel?

- We learn that joy is a risk, and also a choice.

- The law of attraction only bring us our desires if they stem from emotional maturity. Emotional immaturity withholds our dreams from us.

- The emotional fork in the road is the choice: stay or grow.

- When we are no longer attached to the path, we know that the detour can be the adventure.

- Our challenging feelings do not define who we are; they reveal the parts of us that need loving.

- Mature emotions may mean moving on, recognizing that all endings prepare us for a new exploration.

LOOKING AHEAD

In the next chapter, we will look at the third chakra and see how our thinking and planning is directly tied to the meaning we have made of our feelings in our second chakra. If we make choices based on how we feel, are we making choices in a mature, supportive manner or an immature, punitive manner? What path will you choose?

THE THIRD CHAKRA (YELLOW): MANIPURA

Lotus: 10 petals

Governance: spleen, small intestine, metabolism

Organs: pancreas, liver

Meaning: intellect

Key Concept: instinct

Western Translation: concentration

Western Color Therapy: choices

Kundalini Aspect: Disciplined thinking is a form of power in yoga, and the practice of higher conscious thinking is what we today call setting an intention.

Herbs and Spice: Cardamom, as both a spice and an essential oil, is a freeing element which liberates the chakra from fear, negativity, self-doubt, and other mental stressors. This facilitates ambition, tenacity, and the achieving of goals.

Third Chakra Physical Challenges

These include pancreatitis, diverticulitis, Crohn's disease, and irritable bowel syndrome (IBS). The challenges in the third chakra can appear around issues of:

- obsessive thinking
- anxiety
- self-hate

Calming the Third Chakra Physical Challenges

Our emotions from the second chakra can trigger the third chakra's instinctual issues around fight or flight.

Below are a few things to journal with to calm your third chakra:

- Fight moves toward, and flight moves away from. What thoughts and the emotions they trigger create either of these actions in you?

- Challenging feelings dissipate when you sit still with them rather than run away. How can this mature emotional stance change your thinking?

- Write. Pretend your anxiety is speaking. What does it want to tell you?

Third Chakra Personal Challenges

When we trace destructive decisions, they will lead us back to mature versus immature feelings as the root cause.

Obsessive thinking when challenged by someone else is often met with an emotional tantrum, which can occur as blame.

For example: During a reading with a client, I inquired if she had challenges in relationships. She reverted to a childlike tone as she replied that she might as well quit right now, because she was never going to get what she wanted.

It can be very challenging to be the receiver of immature communication.

I lovingly agreed with her: *she should quit if that's what felt like a solid choice to her.*

My unwillingness to engage with emotional immaturity opened the door for her to see her immature emotional pattern, and we were able to explore how to guide her second chakra's emotions into more mature communication.

You can do it for yourself by remembering: There is always a brief moment (before an upset) where your third chakra can intervene by asking: *Is this a mature, uplifting decision?*

Can you see where this would serve you well in your second chakra emotions and third chakra thinking process?

CRYSTALS AND STONES OF THE THIRD CHAKRA

The crystals for the third chakra are said to soothe and clear the chakra to support clear thinking and address issues of low self-esteem and powerlessness.

Crystals that support the third chakra include:

- **Lemon quartz:** Considered the financial abundance stone, it also alleviates obsession around food and can aid in digestive disorders.

- **Yellow tourmaline:** A rare stone—so powerful it is said to rid one of negative influences—it is a natural purifying energy.

- **Citrine:** It is a remover of negative influences in relationships, as it dispels negative energy. It is one of the few stones that does not need to be cleansed.

- **Yellow jasper:** This stone stimulates clarity and focus.

- **Amber:** This is the stone of purpose and elevated thinking.

- **Tiger's eye:** It supports keeping our eye on what needs to be guarded; a protective stone while traveling.

> **THE COLOR YELLOW**
> Yellow is related to the way we think, plan, and our natural response to our fight or flight instinct.

If it is easier to imagine the color yellow than your third chakra, do that as you explore the third chakra.

CHAKRA COLOR: YELLOW

- **Attributes:** creative, intelligent, precise, cooperative, reasonable, innovative, original, instinctual, wise

- **Statement:** Let your instinct be your guide.

- **Impression:** reasoning

EVOLUTION OF MEANING

In Eastern practices, as one evolves in a chakra one ascends to the next one. A common third chakra practice is to focus on one's breathing. This personal discipline is a practice in stillness and quieting the mind.

The adaptation in our modern definition is where practicality and discipline meet. Our mental focus is the way in which we operate in our third chakra in everyday life. Becoming aware of our mature feeling state, or our immature emotional state, is where we can begin to recognize how our thoughts in fact begin in the prior chakra.

MODERN INTERPRETATION

Manifesting, the law of attraction, and goal setting are relatively modern concepts. The Eastern yogis had little need to focus on a new home, job, or relationship. Yet using the principles of the third chakra becomes extremely powerful in manifesting as it relates to mental discipline and focus. Facing whatever we encounter and staying the course is energy associated with this chakra of instinctual thought.

GOAL VERSUS INTENTION

These two modern ideas reside here in the third chakra:

First, an intention is not a goal. A goal is who you become in the process of achieving it; as in when you reach your goal of going to medical school and finishing your residency you will be a doctor. And it is who you become on the journey that constitutes a goal.

An intention is bigger than a wish and more intense than a goal.

An intention is the force that rolls determination and spirit all into one and throws it out into the universe like a meteor, hurtling it toward creation and manifestation.

This is the power of your intention and chakra combined.

THE SOLAR PLEXUS STORY

While teaching a class on the third chakra, I asked for a volunteer to share a painful moment from their childhood.

Many enlightened adults will lead any painful memory with: "I've accepted it" or "I can't really blame my parents anymore..."

A confident, outspoken woman spoke up: "I was abandoned by my mother."

Everyone in the room nodded their understanding.

Others in the room were unsettled when I asked her to explain what "abandonment" meant. She responded, in a tone that revealed her executive role in life, "Oh come on, Tori. You know what abandonment means."

I knew what abandonment meant. But I didn't know what it meant to *her*. I was inquiring as to what happened that she concluded she was abandoned by her mother.

She told us: "When I was a kid, I would come home from school every day, and my mother would have her back to me, and simply point to the dining room and say, 'Your snack is on the table, take it inside and go do your homework.' She never turned to look at me, or come talk to me. She completely abandoned me."

Her father worked nights and she never saw him. When she left for school in the morning, he would still be sleeping.

We sat quietly for a time. Thinking. There is a natural energy in stillness, in allowing space of thought. For some it quiets the mind. For others, it creates discomfort.

Anxious vibes were building in the room.

Then, in a childlike voice, she added, "I really don't care either way because he used to beat my mother and I hated him. And no, I never heard or saw anything."

I wondered how she knew that her father beat her mother if she never saw her father or heard anything.

She bristled, and to hold back other opinions in the room, I held my hand up asking them to wait for her reply. "How did you know you were abandoned?"

There was a long silence, and then her head fell into her hands, she took a deep breath, and her eyes welled up. "Oh my God, my mother was trying to protect me from seeing her bruises."

That was my sense of it as well. Her mother probably had fresh bruises each day and didn't want her daughter to witness them.

Her entire life had been wired around this belief that she had been abandoned. And in the history she told us, she had been abandoned by every man she had ever been in a relationship with. Her belief had created a feeling she was trying to get over—and her focus on abandonment created it over and over again. Once she integrated the story with a new perspective, her outcome would change.

She described feeling lightheaded, warm, and completely detached, yet in the same moment free and relieved. At the same time, she began to shiver.

She was experiencing a raising of her consciousness. Her immature feelings in her second chakra had risen to a mature understanding in her third chakra. This kind of awakening promises that everything in her life would change in that moment.

She now knew that her mom was protecting, not abandoning her. Knowing she was loved was more powerful than the belief she had been abandoned.

The emotional meaning she made as an eight-year-old had dictated her entire life. Once the meaning changed, her entire life changed. Today she is in a long-term relationship with her partner.

This is an example of a modern use of chakra healing and of how trusting your instinct takes place in the third chakra.

MEDITATION

As we look at our third chakra—thoughts and plans—we can easily see how often decisions are based on our feelings. This is the discipline of the second chakra, as we learned the difference between immature and mature feelings.

In your mind's eye, take a moment to imagine the bridge between your second and third chakra. With soft focus eyes, continue reading and notice that when a feeling takes us into upset, the message is sent across the bridge to our third chakra where our thinking, and perhaps our ego, take over.

I'm going to invite you to stand on that bridge and observe a strong feeling from the second chakra coming toward you on one side.

Now hold your hand up to stop it, and imagine in this moment the discipline that the yogis used in containing their inner cobra.

Breathe.

As you are holding this energy back, allow the feeling in your hand to be localized in the center of your palm.

Breathe again. And this time, exhale the feeling out to the universe, which is bigger and wider and can take this feeling and transform it to one of love and wisdom.

And now begin to lower your hand. In your own stillness, allow the feeling to wash over you and move past you into your third chakra.

Now turn and walk into your third chakra, crossing the bridge.

As you arrive on the other side, decide if this feeling is creating a higher or lower vibration in your third chakra. Is it elevating you to the highest possible conscious thought or is it lowering you into upset?

Go ahead and drop your shoulders; come back into your

waking consciousness. This entire exercise can be done in the span of the time it takes to go from an emotional storm to a split-second decision that can determine the focus of your life.

You have now experienced the discipline necessary to contain the energy of your third chakra to make it usable and applicable on your personal map.

THOUGHTS AND THE THIRD CHAKRA: YOUR INTERNAL MAP

"Thinking in general is fed from two sources,
firstly from subjective and in the last resort un-
conscious roots, and secondly from objective data
transmitted through sense perceptions."

—Carl Jung

Let's take a look at this STOP on your internal chakra map

Have you ever signed up for a class you are very excited about, and after the second week, you quit? Or you suddenly stopped going? Or you ran out of desire to participate?

Most people will drop out of a class between their second and third week. As you discovered in the meditation, the discipline necessary in the second chakra is often overlooked, causing most people to give up their dreams somewhere on the bridge between the second and third chakra.

Our emotions flare up, and if they are guiding our third chakra of planning and thought, all it takes for us to quit is a feeling that stops us. Negative feelings will override good feelings and drive us to quit.

One way to transform this is to tap into the discipline available in your third chakra. Next time you want to quit, simply say to yourself: *Boy, this feeling IS painful, but I'm going to do it anyway.*

Or another idea is to procrastinate a desire to quit by telling yourself: *This feeling of wanting to quit is vital and highly important. It is very strong, and one that I really need to look at . . . tomorrow. I will think about it tomorrow and for now, I will show up anyway.*

Then decide: *I will make no plans until this feeling passes, and until I am certain that quitting or walking away is for my highest good.*

These thoughts combined with action are a powerful discipline of the third chakra.

WHEN YOUR THIRD CHAKRA IS UNSETTLED, LOOK TO THE PRIOR ONE

One of the things to really keep in mind is that lower vibrational thinking can bring us to a place we truly don't want to end up, yet it starts with unsafe or frightening feelings. Again, if we look at the challenging side of a chakra, it is directly related to lower vibrational thinking in the prior chakras. How we feel is going to dictate plans we will or won't make in our life.

> *Our thoughts are like a steering wheel. Only you can decide who is in the driver's seat of your life.*

WRITE ABOUT IT

The Antonym Approach / 7 minutes

In this chakra, we're going to use the antonyms in a different way. What if you could take a feeling that YOU know has stopped you from creating breakthroughs in your life, and the next time it comes up, you will have devised ways to transform what once stopped you?

Let's look at the way defeating feelings may affect you on a daily basis.

- Take a few minutes to list out all the feelings that are familiar to you that stop or diminish you.

- There is nothing you need to do about them—simply make the list.

- Next, look up the antonyms and write those down next to each emotion listed.

- Write the word (or words) on an index card and on the other side write the word that opposes it.

- The next time a disempowering feeling overcomes you, pull out your card OR create a new one in the moment.

Keywords and Phrases That Relate to the Third Chakra

- **Keywords:** willpower, self-confidence, self-control, purpose, desire, vitality, willpower, gut instinct, low intuition, details, mental, anger, instinct, ego

- **Key Phrases:** Let me think about it, follow the yellow brick road, this is the way I think, what you think about you bring about, thoughts are things, striving for perfection

MANIFESTING INTENTION

Your inner guide emerges. In the third chakra of yellow, we turn our porch light on and let our angels know we are home. It is time to decide if you will allow the magic in.

Third Chakra Key Ideas

- When we give up being who we are not, we open the door to who we are.

- Fears are challenges that we integrate through mature emotions on the path to enlightenment.

- We must face dilemmas with dignity.

- When we ignore our feelings, we are destined to be ruled by them.

- The solution is always simple when we surrender our attachment to an outcome.

- Wise choices mean thinking in an expansive way.

- Your feelings can no longer dictate what you will or will not take action on.

LOOKING AHEAD

In the next chapter, we will look at the fourth chakra and see how whether our heart is invested in a plan or not is directly related to our third chakra.

The reality is that in our fourth chakra we open our heart, and there are times when our thinking can override what is good for us. Therefore, when you are faced with heartbreak, it is only a matter of time before you are able to see where the red flags were. This is a common way our thinking overrides our better judgment.

THE FOURTH CHAKRA (GREEN): ANAHATA

Lotus: 12 petals

Governance: thymus gland

Organs: heart

Meaning: opening

Key Concept: matters of the heart

Western Translation: compassion

Western Color Therapy: harmony

Kundalini Aspect: As the energy rises in kundalini, we are now opening to the vast expanse of the fourth chakra and the energy of love. When the first three chakras are open through awareness it opens the door to ascension into the heart chakra.

Herbs and Spices: *basil, sage, and thyme.* The herbs here are chosen because they are good for the physical heart. All herbs and spices to strengthen and heal the heart itself can be used in personal rituals to honor love in our lives.

The life we create in the first three chakras determines whether our internal cobra is serving us, or we are serving it.

Fourth Chakra Physical Challenges

These include acid reflux, arrhythmia, chronic obstructive pulmonary disease (COPD), asthma, and pneumonia. Challenges in the fourth chakra appear around issues of:

- exhaustion
- grief
- resentment

Calming the Fourth Chakra Physical Challenges

The fourth chakra calls for compassionate self-care and awareness. The heart is gentle and can create confusion when spiritually exhausted. The most powerful space may be meditation. Remember, a nap is meditative time too. Allow yourself to rest.

Fourth Chakra Personal Challenges

Jealousy, hatred, anger, and loneliness are fourth chakra challenges.

During a class I was teaching, Sally, one of the participants, admitted that she felt the most angst about the fourth chakra. Her family of origin was a scream fest, and more than once it had escalated to violence. I commented that she was probably great in a crisis. Startled, she admitted she was a crisis counselor. She had won awards, and set up programs for families in crisis.

Calming the Fourth Chakra Personal Challenges

One of the key components of the fourth chakra is compassion. The compassion Sally had for those she guided was unmatched. Yet she had little for herself.

Her decision was to rest, and to find activities where she was not a leader, but a participant and student. She decided to do solo pursuits in a class setting; knitting was perfect for her. She could not only relax in the class, but learn from others more experienced than she.

CRYSTALS AND STONES OF THE FOURTH CHAKRA

Crystals that open, activate, and soothe the fourth chakra include:

- **Green aventurine:** This stone brings tranquility and is thought to open the heart to creativity.

- **Green:** compassion.

- **Rose quartz:** This is one of the most common crystals for love, as it offers the vibrational aspect of compassion; frequently used to heal a heart that has been hurt.

- **Green calcite:** This semiprecious stone is related to blood flow in the heart and is frequently used in money attraction spells as it is thought to remove impediments.

- **Jade:** This semiprecious stone guides in opening your heart to a higher purpose; an excellent meditation stone.

Note: At some frequencies the fourth chakra may appear pink, and in some chakra books you may see the color pink attributed to the fourth chakra; this color variation represents the higher vibration of the chakras seen at some angles.

> *"Your visions will become clear only when you can look into your own heart. Who looks outside, dreams; who looks inside, awakes."*
>
> —Carl Jung

CHAKRA COLOR: GREEN

The color green itself represents growth, life, and love and brings calm to an environment. As the color of nature, it is a seed of compassion.

> *If it is easier to visualize the color green than to imagine your fourth chakra, do that until the chakra resonates with you.*

- **Attributes:** balance, harmony, brotherhood, hope, growth, healing, love, peace, prosperity
- **Statement:** Anything is possible with an open heart.
- **Impression:** love

EVOLUTION OF MEANING

In some yoga practices, the fourth chakra means "unstuck." This chakra is the bridge between the physical body of the first three chakras and the spiritual body of the final three. As we become unstuck from our earthly desires, we progress toward spiritual bliss. The fourth chakra is the true guardian between the physical and the unseen.

MODERN INTERPRETATION

The ability to be active in fulfilling our own desires, or to release an unconscious obligation that we are playing out in our life, mirrors the idea of spiritual obedience used in the Eastern disciplines from long ago.

Chakra use today often includes manifesting our desires, which is another way of saying law of attraction work. What is overlooked is the idea that it takes work (energetic discipline) to awaken your chakras.

People often jump from the third chakra (idea) of their plan—skipping the fourth chakra—into that fifth chakra of manifesting.

If you have a hidden motive, or are not fully standing in integrity, you may get stopped in the fourth chakra. Inquiring with a curious nature is the kindness necessary to open our heart chakra. Ultimately the heart asks for the truth, and when we fulfill that within ourselves, we can ascend to the next chakra.

THE HEART STORY

I was teaching a "Manifesting with the Chakra" class, and each participant shared what they wanted to manifest.

Kate was in the process of opening her own bakery. Her favorite memory growing up was her mother's family bakeshop. She loved going to the store every day after school, doing her homework, and delighting in one of the special baked goods that her grandmother had made. It was the happiest time from her childhood.

When the store closed during her teen years, it became her life's mission to re-create that experience.

By the time she joined my class, she was well on her way to manifesting her dream. She had a business plan, a pending loan application, and an ideal spot in a seaside resort town. She was about to sign the lease when she heard about the class. She registered to give herself some solid direction in manifesting and energizing with her chakras. In the first week, she was excited to share her intentions.

By week two, she admitted that she had been up and down emotionally. A few of the participants in the class assured her that her feelings were normal.

As this was the second week, we were working with the second chakra. While I validated her feelings, I was careful not to offer a solution. Remember fear can bubble up in the second chakra, and thoughts can turn quickly to wanting to quit.

When we are creating our own manifesting map, the tendency can be to ask directions when we have our destination already. This is especially true when we are learning to read our map.

Staying on track is a matter of refocusing your feelings on what you truly desire and, even though you feel fear, following the idea of *doing it anyway.*

By week three she admitted thinking, in her own words, "that this was all kinds of wrong."

There is a vast difference between forcing yourself to do something and really desiring something and experiencing jitters. I reminded her that she could change her mind if she wanted to. She swiftly entered a state of emotional upset.

It was her dream—what she really wanted!

Some of the participants began suggesting that this was a block in her third chakra, and perhaps her instinct was telling her something.

She reiterated how important this bakery was, and how vital it was for others to be able to have the wonderful memories she had.

Sometimes when we pursue a dream to re-create a memory, it may be to make someone else happy. Our soul wants to prove that, through our actions, the family can revert back to a happier time.

I asked her to clarify her thought process: Is this your dream, or is it a dream that you think you must accomplish because of someone else?

A deep sadness overcame her. She left class crying that day.

In the fourth week, she was noticeably absent. To her credit, she returned in the fifth week and admitted that she really didn't want a bakery.

Her mother wasn't the best businessperson. Kate's degree was in business management. Losing the bakery destroyed her family. It was the heart of her family . . . soon after the bakery closed, her grandmother and grandfather passed away. She paused.

It wasn't her dream; it was a decision made as a teenager that she was going to repair her family. In reality, she simply lacked the tools to deal with the deaths of her grandparents.

In a lightning moment she blurted out: "Heart attacks. They had heart attacks within three months."

In recognizing that her heart was in grief and that she really didn't want the bakery, she found her path to truly opening her heart to what was important to her. The week between the fourth and fifth chakra had given the space to let her heart grieve for the love she never grieved at the time.

In week five she had changed her intention to wanting to meet a partner with whom she could share a dream—whatever that might look like.

By recognizing the truth in her heart, she opened a route to finding joy again and a space for her soul to grow. And for her joy meant meeting a widower with two children and opening a restaurant, and it was where her open heart truly belonged.

By being willing to give up what we think (third chakra) we want, our heart (fourth chakra) opens to a higher awareness and we become able to step into our true destiny.

Since grief is love without a place to go, we often need to grieve the loss of a dream before stepping into a new one.

MEDITATION

What follows is an experiential meditation, and as you read the words on the page, allow your inner wise soul to keep soft eyes as you embark on this journey.

To fully experience the fourth chakra, let's bring down some white light from the heavens and, as it filters down into the space where you are now, allow it to come in through the top of your head and filter down to your heart, resting and filling it with light.

At the same time, another peaceful white light is surrounding you and coming up through your root chakra, into your feet and climbing up, enveloping your root chakra and ascending to your second chakra. And as this light from below reaches your third chakra, it connects with the light from heavens, and they meet in your heart chakra.

Allow this calming light to remain as long as you like. And when you are ready . . .

. . . In your mind's eye, imagine your heart chakra is akin to the top of a mountain in the fall. Your heart is open and flourishing, and as you look over the side of the mountain, the leaves on the trees are red, orange, and yellow; and they will return to the earth, for these grounding earthly chakras represent physical, living, breathing energy.

The nature of our journey has been to reach the opening at which we now stand. This is the final grounding point and launchpad into your unseen spiritual body chakra. The true intention of our heart chakra is to allow that which is below to rise up into the highest spiritual peaks available to us before we move into the spiritual realm of communication, expression, manifesting, and, if successful, the true experience of our God consciousness.

Balance is a myth created by our Western thinking. And no-where is this more clear than in our fourth chakra of the heart, perfectly situated in the middle of our seven chakra system. Many people mistakenly believe that if we are balanced, we will be happy.

The idea of balance is an ideal.

Imagine a seesaw. Perfectly balanced. Yet we cannot stay here. This peace and perfection is meant to be shared. Our heart chakra craves connection! That is what this conduit is. We connect our plans and thoughts with our voice, as it flows up through the purity of our heart.

So while the discipline of holding balance is lovely, it is not intended to be held, but rather experienced, thus allowing us to evolve through the fourth chakra into sharing with others. Balance must only be held for a time, like breath in yoga, and then released. Then in the fifth chakra it sends our message out to the world.

When you are ready, bring your awareness back to your waking consciousness, having met and experienced your fourth chakra.

Perfection Will Stop Us in the Fourth Chakra

"The tree that does not bend with the wind will be broken by the wind."

—Chinese proverb

The fourth chakra is a true lesson in the resilience of our heart. While we know intellectually that our heart can't "attack" us, it is here that we open our heart, knowing the risk.

Define love. Share love. See love everywhere, not simply in the form we demand of the universe.

APPLYING THE FOURTH CHAKRA:
YOUR MAP HAS YOUR ANSWERS

Remember: your answers are already inside you.

We must risk being in balance or out of balance, having the courage to love, and risk forgiving ourselves with the understanding that we may experience sadness for wasted time or grieve what we ignored. At this point in our chakra map the lesson is one of courage.

Our heart must connect us to the true nature of spirit in our higher selves, and what comes forward is the gratitude that lives in the fourth chakra and opens our heart, challenging us to be true to ourselves and our dreams and to honor others' dreams too.

Risk is key.

Where in your life are you courageous?

Everyone is courageous in some area of their life. The part of our map where we choose the town, highway, freeway, or autobahn we will travel is our personal path; this is determined in the fourth chakra.

WHEN YOUR FOURTH CHAKRA IS UNSETTLED,
LOOK TO THE PRIOR ONE

It is in the third chakra that a plan is formed. If our heart is not invested in this plan, it will often show up as a lack of momentum, or an odd sense of disinterest in carrying out our plan. Being true to ourselves, and following our heart, begins with an authentic plan. When we make decisions based on a pure desire, our heart opens.

CHAKRA EXERCISE/WRITE ABOUT IT

An Intuitive Exercise: The Synonym Approach / 4 minutes

1. Make a list. Write down as fast as you can the things, feelings, or experiences that have opened your heart to massive joy.

Go!

2. Next, look to the keywords or phrases (listed below) that apply to your list. Apply ONE phrase or keyword to each item on your list.

3. Now, go look up a list of synonyms that relate to the word you chose. If you chose *joy*, for example, look at all the synonyms and pick the one that resonates with you in the moment.

4. The word you chose is a special message for you around your deepest desire. It will relate to the one thing that opens your heart.

5. If you have one, use one of the fourth chakra gemstones and ask your own internal wisdom to let you know what this word means.

6. Let it go; allow yourself a few days to process this experience without expectations.

Keywords and Phrases That Relate to the Fourth Chakra

- **Keywords:** heart, compassion, love, connection, caring, joy, patience, peace, kindness

- **Key Phrases:** my heart isn't in it, her heart was in the right place, having compassion for others, integration of community, you're going to give me a heart attack, his heart is closed

MANIFESTING INTENTION

I will stay open to new opportunities to give and receive love. I declare myself ready to stay open to vibes my heart picks up on. I will act only when I feel peace, and know what is in my heart.

Fourth Chakra Key Ideas

- Is the path we choose (or chose) honestly what our heart desires?

- Experiencing sadness may be part of the road to personal integrity.

- We honor our personal growth as necessary.

- An open heart may change our perception.

- Grief is love without a place to go.

LOOKING AHEAD

In the next chapter, we will look at the fifth chakra and how what we manifest has flowed through our heart chakra. Whatever your heart is committed to will show up in your life. Conversely, if what you say you desire does not align with your heart chakra, what shows up in your life may disappoint you.

The fifth chakra reveals what you will and won't manifest, based on the messages you send out to the world.

THE FIFTH CHAKRA (BLUE): VISHUDDHA

Lotus: 16 petals

Governance: thyroid, metabolism, and body temperature

Organs: vocal cords, mouth, tongue and esophagus, bronchial tubes, respiratory system

Meaning: purification

Key Concept: communication

Western Translation: creative expression

Western Color Therapy: truthful dialogue with others

Kundalini Aspect: Spiritual confidence rises as we are now ready to speak our truth. We step into higher levels of discernment as this chakra gives voice to our heart's desires.

Herbs and Spices: *red clover blossoms, lemon balm.* These are herbs related to the clearing and soothing of the throat. Spices that are used to heal your throat would be considered to have restorative energy for the fifth chakra.

Fifth Chakra Physical Challenges

These include thyroid dysfunction, bronchial and esophageal issues, respiratory problems. Physical challenges in the fifth chakra stem from internal issues of:

- childhood wounds
- shame
- verbal abuse

Calming the Fifth Chakra Physical Challenges

Many healers say we are responsible for everything in our lives, and while that may be true, telling someone that they asked for an ailment may prevent them from wanting to look at how their own energy attracted it.

In essence, the fifth chakra represents how the world perceives and responds to you; it is directly related to what you physically manifest in your life. It is a reminder that our mission in life may be bigger than we are, and a dis-ease may be related to a bigger request the universe is granting.

Fifth Chakra Personal Challenge

The biggest challenge by far is trying to stay small and therefore invisible to avoid judgment or humiliation. As the fifth chakra is the manifesting chakra, the law of attraction is switched on, and could reinforce an experience of not getting what you say you want.

Calming the Fifth Chakra Personal Challenges

To change the dynamic of not being heard and being unable to ask for what you want, write down as thoroughly as you can what exactly keeps repeating in your world.

- Write down what you observe—keep it brief. Do not explain. ONLY write the experience. For example: waiters always ignore me.

- Next, tell a story. If YOU were a waiter and saw you at a table, how would you respond? Do not tell it from your point of view at all, only describe what the *waiter* sees.

- Share it with a friend who will not try to fix or judge you.

If need be, have your friend help you edit out ALL the emotional charge in your writing. Now, as impartially as you can, what message would you need to send out to create what is happening?

What would be the opposite message?

CRYSTALS AND STONES OF THE FIFTH CHAKRA

The following crystals and stones are associated with, and used for, throat chakra healing:

- **Amazonite:** These are crystals in various shades of blue used to foster emotional balance and repel negativity.

- **Azurite:** This mineral in contrasting shades of blue is known for balancing the throat chakra and supporting our voice in pursuit of our higher self.

- **Turquoise:** A semiprecious blue or blue-green stone, it is used to promote confident and effective communication.

- **Blue topaz:** This stone focuses healing spiritual energy to repair and support the body.

- **Lapis lazuli:** This blue semiprecious stone is also known as the "stone of truth" for its use in promoting effective communication.

- **Aquamarine:** Ranging from green-blue to blue, this cleansing semiprecious stone fosters tolerance and empathy while quelling fears.

CHAKRA COLOR: BLUE

The key concept of the fifth chakra is sound and hearing.

- **Attributes:** truth, communication, loyalty, serenity, faith, spirituality, creativity, expression
- **Statement:** You will manifest your precise communication to the universe.
- **Impression:** visionary

It is much easier to experience the color blue than to imagine your fifth chakra.

EVOLUTION OF MEANING

If we look closer at the evolution here, in Eastern studies it is communication of the divinity within and our connection to it that matters the most. It is not a big stretch to see the power assigned to the fifth chakra is a significant indicator of whether we will be truthful with ourselves, the universe, and others. When we're connected with the highest aspect of a particular chakra, we are in fact connected to the divine within.

While energy healers will work to clear this chakra, and meditation can calm it, our communication must be a clear channel, or the issues of our past will cloud our future. This chakra requires clarity in our expression. In many ways it is in the fifth chakra that our success and failure in life is revealed through our clarity or lack thereof.

MODERN INTERPRETATION

The fifth chakra will reflect who you are and therefore what you will attract to the world. As the law of attraction stipulates, who we are is seen, and like attracts like. This is where the modern idea of manifesting our dreams becomes possible and will require complete focus.

One of the misnomers here is the thinking that manifesting what we deeply desire is easy; and while that is true to some degree, if you are not in touch with your heart's truth, what you receive may not be what you truly desire; think of it as ordering coffee when you meant milk and being surprised that you received coffee.

The structured discipline of chakra evolution entails truly knowing yourself and being able to speak your truth, which makes manifesting appear easy for some people.

Someone who is afraid to ask for a raise from their boss is not speaking their truth, and therefore they are out of alignment in their fifth chakra.

You may know someone who practices yoga, and while they have mastered their physicality quite exquisitely, they may have an inability to translate this physical discipline into their everyday communication. Which may include an unconscious vow of poverty, excessive drug or alcohol use, or not asking for a raise, and when we look at it that way it becomes clear that the real world is beyond the four walls and requires a form of intimacy* that can frighten someone who does not comprehend the power of their chakras.

Are you seeing the value of the chakras as they build your internal map inside?

> *Intimacy is IN-TO-ME-SEE—it is not what we get from others, it is rather who we are. People can see who you are, and whether they like you or not, they see you clearly.

This is one of the primary reasons that the modern chakra system can transform our lives. We have within us all the ability that the monks had centuries ago; the missing element is often discipline.

Let's switch gears and take a look at what I like to call communication amnesia (a hidden agenda), when we do not create what we say we want; the outcome is a cycle of blaming other people for the outcome we do get.

Ignored Communication = Placing Blame on Others

THE THROAT STORY

Knowing your own darkness is the best method for dealing with the darknesses of other people.

—Carl Jung

I often say, the only way out is through. Translation? In order for us to evolve, tough conversations must be had. While the story below may appear to be a way to "blame the victim," I'm going to ask you to suspend judgment. I do encourage you to validate any personal upset (should it occur) and allow yourself to look to the opportunity we each have to transform our own method of communication at any time.

Do your best to see the point of the story rather than allowing it to make a point around societal victimization of women. While that has been a truth in history, this story's purpose is to indicate an internal shift that can be made to allow us to clear and live into our authenticity through our fifth chakra.

Okay, ready?

A few years back I was leading a chakra mastermind group in Los Angeles focusing on creating relationships in the industry (entertainment). It was an eight-week workshop and two of the participants were a husband and wife business team.

She was an actress, he was a writer, and she was looking for a producer/director to package their project—with her as the lead actress—and take it to a major studio. What they needed was to create connections to make their dream a reality. For Janie and her husband, it was to attract a partner to champion their work.

They went to a high-level networking event where Janie met a very prominent producer/director. The following week she enthusiastically reported that she and this man spoke for over an hour about spirituality and God and had a real connection. When he suggested meeting for lunch the following week, she was excited.

After their lunch, she showed up in our group visibly upset and quite angry. His interest was not in her script, but rather in inviting her back to his hotel. She was hurt and embarrassed over his hidden agenda.

When he made his move, she was taken aback; she thought they were going to talk about her movie. His response was that he didn't need her movie—he could make any movie he wanted. He was clearly interested in something else. She was crushed.

Everyone in the group agreed that *he* had a hidden agenda and had lured her to lunch under a false pretense.

While this part was true, it was important that we take on the communication here for evolution.

On some level, Janie knew the spiritual talk was a fake connection. She chose to see that she was moving closer to her dream rather than admitting that the conversation she had with this man to begin with was superficial. To support her intention (third chakra) to get her movie made, she skipped over her heart (fourth chakra) and instead created a connection riddled with hidden agendas. What she missed was *her own* hidden agenda.

When things didn't turn out as she'd hoped, she held someone else's bad behavior responsible for her dream not coming true.

> Unfortunately, if we ignore our fifth chakra and ignore what we internally know isn't working for us, it will often come back to us in the form of our feeling that someone else has betrayed us.

In all fairness, he knew what she wanted, and he let her play out her scheme in front of him. The challenge is that it becomes about who is *more* deceptive, and not about how we can change our behavior to create the outcome we desire.

Remember: What you skip stops you.

She was upset by what she perceived to be his hidden agenda, but couldn't see her own—to get love and admiration from the public.

She expressed that the movie was vital, and it meant so much to her. The truth was she wanted it to make her famous so that she could get love and admiration from strangers. What the universe sent back was a mirror of her deepest desire.

Think about it. This man offered fake love and admiration. The real issue was that it did not come in the form that she wanted. However, it was a mirror.

She was sitting there at lunch with a stranger who could make her famous. Notice how that word *stranger* illuminates how this situation played out?

As the saying goes: *What you think about, you bring about.* This saying is true. The danger lies in skipping the heart chakra, and in reality we do this to camouflage a hidden agenda. When we talk about the vibes we are sending out to the universe, this is where they originate.

> When communications from the fifth chakra are vague, personal vision is also unclear. An imbalanced chakra can feel, energetically, as if you are being held back from something you truly desire.

EPILOGUE

A clear fifth chakra is revealed in those who manifest quickly, and is a result of the fluid connection between the fourth and fifth chakras.

Your fifth chakra is the vibrational energy you are always sending out to the world. Therefore the way to see what is going on within your fifth chakra is to look at the reality of your life.

Are you single or married? The vibrational energy from your fifth chakra is exactly what creates your relationships.

Are you in a job you like or dislike? Again even without your conscious mind at work, the vibration you are sending out into the world is what shows up.

EXPERIENTIAL MEDITATION

Once again, I am going to ask you to read this with soft focus as you allow yourself to be present and read the words as your eyes cross the page.

Do not follow me; rather listen in your mind as you read to yourself. The fifth chakra is your manifesting chakra. This is the place in which everything that you are experiencing, have experienced, and will experience in the future is decided.

Breathe.

> An energetic vibrational trance can take many forms. For example, a trance or state occurs when we are shopping, cooking, working out, or at play.

You are already in a state of awareness, and this meditative state is connecting you directly with your fifth chakra.

As you read this, you may be trying to understand what you are reading. Let go if you are trying to understand a meditation that has already begun. We are going to bypass your logical thinking.

Now bring the white light down from the heavens to create a nice soft angelic presence embracing you. As this energy swirls around you, begin to recognize that it is illuminating your throat chakra. The color blue is vibrating around, within, and from your fifth chakra. Can you see it in your mind's eye?

Breathe.

The light you are seeing around your throat chakra is the current manifesting energy that you are sending out. As you look around the room or space you are currently seated in, become aware that, with invisible effort, you have energetically created everything in your world.

This soft blue emanating from your throat is the invisible energy force that, as you strengthen it and become more aware of it, becomes a powerful manifesting vibrational tool. Notice where this blue light is and how far it flows from your throat chakra before fading.

The current blue vibration is all you need to create what you have in your life to this point.

This blue light is your connection to spirit.

You can step into this meditative state at any time, take your deepest desire, place it directly in front of you, send your manifesting fifth chakra light around it, and send it out to the world of creation.

This is what master manifestors do subconsciously. You now know how to do it consciously.

Allow yourself to recognize the power of your fifth chakra energy. When you are ready, come back to your fully conscious state once again. Bring with you the conscious awareness of this meditative state and you can access it at any time.

FIFTH CHAKRA: YOUR MAP HAS YOUR ANSWERS

How come I'm not getting what I really desire?

You may be creating internal belief blockers. This is resistance inside one of your chakras, which occurs when you create one belief to circumvent another belief.

As you begin to work with these principles, you may find that your results are not as immediate as you might have hoped. This is where we borrow from Eastern discipline and look at our chakra challenges as part of our map in a particular chakra and not a dead end.

You are always attracting the truth of who you are. If you feel less than, even if you recite a million affirmations, what you desire will elude you.

Your inner reality will always manifest your outer reality.

WHEN YOUR FIFTH CHAKRA IS UNSETTLED, LOOK TO THE PRIOR ONE

Unfortunately if we ignore our fourth chakra—meaning ignore what we sense isn't working for us—it will often come back to us in our fifth chakra in the form of a feeling that someone else has betrayed us.

What comes from our heart gets expressed into the world.

If anything is withheld in the heart chakra, it will create communication issues that threaten to become lies and deceit.

"We do not attract what we want, but what we are."

—James Allen

This is the natural flow between you and what shows up in your life. In essence, as Jung said, the connection between the seen and unseen world is accepted as real or it stops here.

A FIFTH CHAKRA INSIGHT

Synchronicity reveals the meaningful connections between the subjective and objective world.

—Carl Jung

CLARITY OF THE UNSPOKEN MESSAGE

We activate the fifth chakra through setting an intention, and our fifth chakra begins working. This means it is energetically sending out to the universe our exact expression. And THAT is what shows up in our life. That is the law of attraction.

WRITE ABOUT IT

Tap into Your Fifth Chakra by Visualizing It / 7 minutes

In the fourth chakra exercise, you created a list of things that brought you joy. Here, go ahead and choose one thing that you would like to see happen in your life. Write it down.

Choose that one thing that you have secretly dreamed about for a long time. Whether you've expressed it to others or not.

I'd like you to see in your mind's eye an active scene of what it would look like for you if this experience was in your life right now.

The beauty of reading this is there's no pressure in the moment; you can take your time. If creating a picture in your mind is a challenge, simply go back to the idea of the feeling that ignites within you a sense of possibility and enthusiasm, or whatever feeling you are looking for. Now place that experience or feeling in front of you, and hold that energy for 17 seconds.

Reawaken that blue ray of light that came through in your throat meditation, and the scene or feeling you just imagined, and send that vision out in the blue ray of light to the universal consciousness all around you.

Now let it go. The manifesting vibration you just sent out from your throat chakra only requires 17 seconds at a time. When you apply this visualization three times a day, you will draw into your life exactly the experience you have asked for.

Writing out your true intention helps solidify what makes your heart sing.

MANIFESTING REALITY

The Antonym Approach

There are times when things show up in your life and it's not exactly what you want to happen. For example, a young woman decides she's tired of attracting men who have no time for her. She changes her intention to someone who is available and creates it. Unfortunately, the first man she attracts is chronically unemployed.

Oftentimes when something like this happens, it has to do more with a need to recapture what was not given to us as children. So in this woman's case the men in her life had been very successful; they just never paid attention to her.

By using the synonym and antonym concept, you can home in on the feeling you are desperately trying to recapture. Notice I used the word *desperate*? When you discover the deep pain inside, you can look at the way you are framing what you need to heal. Each of the prior chakra chapters and stories have brought you to this place of understanding.

Tip: At any time, you can use one of the visualizations, meditations, or exercises in any chakra. As you can see in the journey you've traveled so far, there may be a few exercises that stand out to you more than others. Remember it is your experience of the chakras that matters, and therefore you can apply any of the exercises to a different chakra if you intuitively feel it will work.

Keywords and Phrases That Relate to the Fifth Chakra

- **Keywords:** expression, creation, manifestation, willpower, responsibility, listening, knowledge

- **Key Phrases:** discover your purpose, express your truth, setting your intention, feeling blue, true blue, is the message being sent the one being received?

MANIFESTING INTENTION

Since you're manifesting every minute, you can simply change directions at any time. The fifth chakra offers you a new definition of personal leadership. While there is discipline involved, it is not necessarily difficult; it simply requires focused intention. Focused intention is key.

Fifth Chakra Key Ideas

- Ignoring what we know to be true is what creates resentment of others.

- False beliefs begin with self-deceit. We begin by knowing that we are manifesting our reality.

- We must focus on truth and clarity to create a reality we desire.

- Can we see our hidden agenda in the words we choose?

- Clear communication may be challenging, yet it is vital to be disciplined in your truth-telling.

- Look to your prior chakras and revisit your internal reality through that lens.

- We can sometimes lose who we are through a belief in a hidden agenda.

LOOKING AHEAD

As the fifth chakra reveals our true manifesting capacity, in the sixth chakra we will get to see what is incomplete with our family of origin. The sixth chakra creates and holds hidden family agreements, our sixth sense, and the window of our past and that of our future.

Completed hidden agreements can play out over and over again if we don't know they are finished.

THE SIXTH CHAKRA (INDIGO): AJNA

Lotus: 2 petals

Governance: pituitary gland

Organs: eyes, sinuses, ears

Meaning: beyond wisdom

Key Concept: universal mind

Western Translation: purpose, spiritual awakening

Western Color Therapy: subconscious mind

Kundalini Aspect: The awakening of spiritual connection and mystical states of higher consciousness. This is the seer who has opened the window to the subtle energy of the universe.

Herbs and Spices: *lavender.* Lavender has long been known as an herb to calm the nerves. As a protection herb, it guards personal health and also promotes clarity of intuitive vision.

Sixth Chakra Physical Challenge

These include headaches, vision problems, insomnia, lack of clarity, and diabetes. Physical challenges in the sixth chakra appear around issues of:

- helplessness
- denial
- regrets

Calming the Sixth Chakra Physical Challenges

In the sixth chakra we are offered a chance to regain our confidence by diving deeper into our intuition—and our intuition speaks to us in cryptic messages.

For example, we all know what the word *trust* means, right? What if I told you that it is also a law? *In the law a trust is a relationship where property is held by one party for the benefit of another party.*

What if your intuition (your sixth sense) is holding your "property"? Did you know property as an attribute means power? So let's look at what the intuitive wisdom of your sixth chakra is doing for you: *The sixth chakra is holding your power until you are ready to use it.*

Are you ready?

Sixth Chakra Personal Challenges

An inability to differentiate your future or past from another person's life or path.

One of the challenges empaths (or sensitives) face is the inability to know where they stop and another person begins. As a challenge it can show up as thinking your survival depends upon energetically connecting, when the opposite may be true.

For example, disconnecting from unsupportive people and their behaviors may be the way to truly thrive in life.

Calming the Sixth Chakra Personal Challenges

Police officers, military personnel, emergency room workers, firefighters, and farmers each must master and learn their craft. Once they master it, they go out and practice. Over time, their instinct and intuitive ability kicks in and they no longer rely upon a book, or try to recall each step, as it has become a cellular memory. The idea of needing to believe in their capability is long gone, and they simply know how to do what they do.

Therefore, the idea that we don't trust or follow our intuition can be discovered simply by knowing that what we focus on most will reveal where we use, and trust, our own intuition.

I had a client at one time who was a highly successful artist yet she consistently doubted her intuition because she made poor relationship choices. Her entire focus and development had been in her career. Once she recognized her intuitive focus was on a different area, she was able to focus her energy on developing her intuitive skills in finding the right partner. Today, using her sharply developed intuition, she has a relationship as successful as her career.

CRYSTALS AND STONES OF THE SIXTH CHAKRA

- **Moldavite:** This stone is thought to have been created by a meteor over 14 million years ago. Its frequency supports spiritual transformation and psychic protection.

- **Black obsidian:** This stone is cooled volcanic lava; it stimulates the third eye, opening you to your internal mystical world, and blocks lies, fears, and illusions.

- **Amethyst:** This semiprecious stone activates intuitive and psychic powers. It vibrates healing frequencies for physical addictions and is known as a mind-body-spirit healing crystal.

- **Purple fluorite:** A purple semiprecious stone, it frees repressed memories that have run our lives, that we may not currently be conscious of.

CHAKRA COLOR: INDIGO

Look to the color indigo to imagine your sixth chakra.

- **Attributes:** intuition, past lives, hidden family agreements, clarity of purpose
- **Statement:** I live in a world of intuitive imagination.
- **Impression:** psychic

The color indigo represents the experiences of your sixth chakra.

EVOLUTION OF MEANING

Some religions surrender to the idea that psychic ability and intuition are evil. In that story, the sixth chakra would be skipped over and we would go from our fifth chakra of communication directly to the God consciousness of the seventh chakra.

The intention of the sixth chakra is to uncover our personal gifts and wounding as we discover our true purpose, and then in the seventh chakra we connect to God consciousness and allow ourselves the bliss of finding our true purpose: to know God within ourselves and others.

> **Ultimately, no matter how we frame it, the true purpose of evolving through the chakras is to find God.**

As more and more people are seeking a deep connection to their heritage and ultimately to the legacy they will leave, the sixth chakra becomes a pivotal point on our personal chakra map that has been missing. When we place the sixth chakra back on the road of our spiritual evolution, we find that empathy for others as well as ourselves is restored.

ACCESSING INTUITIVE MASTERY

I'm a native New Yorker, and the old IRT local trains that ran on the Lexington Avenue line never stopped at the 18th Street station (in Manhattan) during my lifetime. In 1948, they closed the station. However, they didn't close the track that ran through that station even though trains no longer stopped there; you can still see the old station. The train stops at 14th and 23rd streets, but the 18th Street station sits there unused.

The point is that just because you don't use something, or you close it off or try to forget it, does not mean it no longer exists.

The sixth chakra exists on each one of our internal chakra maps. That means we all have psychic ability. Free will dictates that we can use that energy in any way we choose. Whatever you master in your lifetime will own the focus of your sixth chakra.

Our intuitive wisdom exists whether we open the station or not.

MODERN INTERPRETATION

The sixth chakra today still represents that which is unique and misunderstood and what our rational mind does not quite understand. This chakra exists in the world of mysticism and empirical dimensions. They are real if we experience them.

THE HIDDEN AGREEMENT STORY

This is a story of a hidden agreement, discovering it, and being set free.

> Hidden agreements typically skip a generation. That means that while our parents' behavior may scar us, the agreement to heal is with our grandparents.

I had just begun working with hidden family agreements and sixth chakra healing when a woman from a major talent agency was referred to me by her therapist. Knowing her therapist, one of the best, I knew that there was something here that was not visible. She was willing to try chakra healing, since her own therapist suggested it.

The woman, whom I'll call Annie, was distraught. She discovered yet another boyfriend cheating on her, this one a well-known musician. She readily admitted that cheating partners was a pattern for her. Her first marriage ended in divorce after her husband had been unfaithful.

Her second engagement to another high-profile Hollywood man also ended for the same reason, and this was, in her words, the "third strike."

Annie was a very smart woman and, in fairness, had done tons of personal work to break these patterns, but nothing was working.

It was a tough one: Her parents were happily married for over forty years. In therapy she had determined that there was no reason for this pattern, and she was doubly frustrated because her parents were the perfect couple. She had had a good example of a strong healthy marriage.

Annie had stumped all the experts.

According to her, happy marriages ran in her family. All four of her grandparents were happily married for over fifty years. Her father's mother was the only living grandparent. Annie greatly admired the sacrifices this woman had made, and the two women were close.

Her grandmother's best friend had lost her husband during the war. Her grandmother insisted the friend live with them until she got back on her feet. The friend stayed with them nearly twenty-five years, until her death, which came just before Annie's grandfather died.

I asked Annie to get more information from her grandmother. Completely disappointed with our session, she left early. I never thought I would hear from her again.

Two weeks later she was sitting before me. Her grandmother admitted that the woman living with her and her husband was never her best friend. It was her husband's mistress, and her grandfather had told his wife that if she ever told anyone or tried to leave, he would ruin her. So she stayed under the same roof and lived a lie for all those years.

Annie was very angry and confused as to what this had to do with her life.

The sixth chakra is where hidden agreements are and where we come to heal the pain of our grandparents. Deeply locked within our soul, we are imprinted with the idea that if our grand-parents had a better life, our parents would have had a better life and therefore we'll have a better life.

Annie's hidden agreement was to heal the wounds of her grandmother. She played out getting involved with a cheater, dis-covering it, and then leaving of her own free will; her grand-mother had never exercised her own free will. This began to make sense to Annie as she flashed on her grandmother having no career, yet insisting Annie have one, and secretly stashing aside money for her granddaughter's education.

Annie's painful pattern was trying to heal the pain her grandmother experienced in not being able to leave and being trapped in a marriage that was not truthful.

Once Annie saw the pattern, she was desperate to change it.

The truth is that the simple recognition that the agreement is complete, as in Annie's case, allows the pattern to dissipate. Yet there is a lingering upset and a sense of agitation, because we want to get over it.

The most challenging part of this is doing nothing, because for some of us we've done nothing for so long we want to take action. However, what we ignore we are destined to repeat, and once you see and acknowledge it, it becomes another stop on the map of your life.

Hidden agreements also relate to the gifts we've been left from our grandparents. As we recognize the agreements that we've come here to heal, our greatest gifts are also set free.

> **If you can look at your life and see the times you have diverted yourself from success, you will see a hidden family agreement.**

MEDITATION

Discovering Your Purpose Intuitively / 9 minutes

As you read this meditation, step into your inner wise self. Take a deep breath and imagine in your mind's eye a beautiful path in the forest.

As you walk together enjoying this perfect uncharted territory, become aware of your sixth chakra activating. Your brow chakra, which is your third eye, rests between your eyebrows, and from this space I'm going to invite you, as you continue walking, to view that which you see through this third eye.

You can see back into your past, you can see the present, and you can see the future. In this journey meditation, we are going to look back and we are going to look inside.

Take a moment and ask your inner wise self what your greatest wounding is.

Become aware as you ask that the wounding may appear as a feeling, an image, or a memory of someone else's behavior.

Take another deep breath, and as you exhale, bring forward that which has been your greatest wounding.

Write down your wounding.

Whatever comes forward for you will hold within it the gift you are here to share with the world.

Stay with what you wrote down. Allow your awareness to fill in the blanks in time. As you do more chakra work, things will become clear.

EPILOGUE

I once shared this concept with a skeptic. I convinced him to share his wounding, and after a bit of wrangling, he decided it wasn't his, but his blind grandfather's wound. His grandfather had lost his sight in an accident, and his greatest pleasure had been watching movies. This man shared with me how his grandfather would piece together the stories describing every shot, and it created a lifelong bond between the two of them.

Would it surprise you if I told you that this man went on to become an award-winning film editor?

Once I pointed out this association, he recognized that the pain of the grandfather he loved was in fact a traumatic wounding for him, which in turn had become his greatest gift.

Sometimes it is easier to see the injustice of a situation—for example, if this man had hated that his grandfather lost his sight, he might have gone on to become an advocate for the blind.

Anger is going to create a different motivator than love. BOTH are valid; anger is not less than.

Remember: How we relate to the issue IS the issue.

There is always one wound that is a driving force, and it often relates to development around your sixth chakra. It will often be the one thing that you have taken on as part of your personal identity. For example, having a sibling or parent who required constant care can create a doctor or alternative healer.

Every wound creates a distinctive imprint, and in our sixth chakra we will always develop our intuitive skills of survival around the wounding we experienced.

APPLYING THE SIXTH CHAKRA: YOUR MAP HAS YOUR ANSWERS

This is the place where we can stop our journey, and many people do. There is a false contentment when one's dreams have not been realized. There is a reconciling to the past that is never explored or undertaken. For some, the journey concludes here and they can go no further.

> *The mass of men lead lives of quiet desperation.*
> *What is called resignation is confirmed desperation.*
>
> —Henry David Thoreau

This is because the map has ended—and where you will go next is no longer fated. What is off the map is the destiny that you can reach when you ascend from the sixth chakra.

WHEN YOUR SIXTH CHAKRA IS UNSETTLED, LOOK TO THE PRIOR ONE

The intention you set and the message you sent out to the world in your fifth chakra will often reveal unclear or mixed signals, even confusion surrounding why things don't work out for you. It can even occur as a block.

A SIXTH CHAKRA INSIGHT

In the sixth chakra we can recognize, from this highest point within our physical body, that we have in fact taken all of our wounding and turned it into our true purpose in life.

Consider your brain versus intuition.
The brain is the safe road; intuition is the unknown.

Our intuition does live in our sixth chakra. And most people struggle to know the difference between their brain and their intuition. Since your brain is always trying to keep you safe, it will allow you to repeat a known pattern before it will allow you to go into the unknown.

Intuition is key.

One of the things to notice is that all of the discomfort and issues that people will share with you regarding blocks in the chakras are really the indicators of our brain trying to shut down our intuition.

INTUITIVE EXERCISE

The Antonym Approach

Is there a word, phrase, synonym, or antonym that you can apply to your wounding? Go ahead and add that to the wounding you wrote down. Make sure you look up the dictionary·meaning of the word or words that you chose.

Keywords and Phrases That Relate to the Sixth Chakra

- **Keywords:** intuition, insight, inspiration, clairvoyance, visualization, mysticism, clarity, perception
- **Key Phrases:** extrasensory perception, trust your intuition, psychic ability, hidden family agreements, inner wisdom, psychic abilities, emotional intelligence

MANIFESTING INTENTION

Once you determine the experience or feeling you are looking to create, write it down, envision it, hold the vision for 17 seconds, and then send it out through the indigo light into the universe. If it still eludes you, look at your personal wounding, or the hidden family agreements that may be residing in the lower vibrational energy of the sixth chakra.

Sixth Chakra Key Ideas

- Our sixth chakra holds the key to how we direct our intuition.
- You are either living your purpose already, or it is hidden in your chakras.
- Self-doubt is a function of the brain, and does not actually exist in our intuition.

- If every state is a trance, what does the trance of your intuition feel like?

- We never really recover a lost self; we discover the aspect of us that we never knew.

- If we are not manifesting what we deeply desire, there may be a hidden agreement we do not see.

LOOKING AHEAD

If we have the courage to work through our sixth chakra issues, which involve pain and challenge and healing, our courage is rewarded as our gift is sent out to the universe. What comes back to us are opportunities far beyond what we had imagined.

In the next and final chakra chapter, we're going to look at what happens in the energy of the crown chakra, and learn the truth about legacy.

THE SEVENTH CHAKRA
(VIOLET OR NEUTRAL): SAHASRARA

Lotus: 1,000 petals

Governance: nervous system

Organs: pineal gland

Meaning: pure consciousness

Key Concept: intuition

Western Translation: universal ideas

Western Color Therapy: Expansion

Kundalini Aspect: This is intimacy (IN-TO-ME-SEE) with the divine. We awaken to the love the universe has to give us, and surrounds us with love. This is complete bliss. Nirvana.

Herbs and Spices: *valerian.* While valerian is known as a sleep aid, it is also used to ease heart palpitations and bring your energy back into your body.

Seventh Chakra Physical Challenges

These include Parkinson's disease, Alzheimer's, paralysis, epilepsy, multiple sclerosis, and cancer. The ailments of the seventh chakra, interestingly, will be:

- universally unresolved diseases
- afflictions that are commonly known
- require dependence upon others (eventually or ongoing)

Calming the Seventh Chakra Physical Challenges

All of these physical challenges bring forward the idea that it is vital to realize that you are not alone and to find others who share this experience. Support groups are one of the most soothing places to connect with a larger consciousness—remember it may not be for you. It may be for the person sitting next to you.

Seventh Chakra Personal Challenge

An inability to connect with the crown chakra may indicate a lack of connection and empathy for others. Keep in mind that this is a very different experience than feeling cut off.

A lack of connection is a stagnant energy that most often occurs when there is unresolved family anger lingering in the sixth chakra preventing true connection with the divine.

Calming the Seventh Chakra Personal Challenge

The seventh chakra connects us not only to higher consciousness but to universal themes that link all of us. It is in reaching out to connect with the universe, God, Goddess, Higher Power that we calm any disconnected feelings. This is one of the most empowering aspects of the seventh chakra, as a reminder that we are here to connect with the divine, and this is available at any time.

CRYSTALS AND STONES OF THE SEVENTH CHAKRA

- **Selenite:** This stone clears congested energies, lifts awareness to higher planes, compels one to move forward in life, and helps remove stagnation.

- **Clear quartz:** This stone amplifies energy, brings heightened spiritual acuity, and expands consciousness. Used to communicate with guides, it encourages clarity and psychic abilities.

- **Amethyst:** This semiprecious stone facilitates meditation and understanding the root cause of one's imbalance or disease; it helps reveal self-destructive patterns of the ego and is used to heal addictive behavior patterns.

- **Diamond:** This precious stone allows access to divine energies, facilitates connection with higher domains, and promotes truth and vision.

CHAKRA COLOR: VIOLET OR NEUTRAL

- **Attributes:** balance, harmony, brotherhood, hope, growth, healing, love, peace, prosperity
- **Impression:** enlightenment

It may be easier to imagine violet or white light than to imagine your seventh chakra.

EVOLUTION OF MEANING

Neutral tones and their connection with spirit are assigned to the seventh chakra; therefore while the color may be violet on the rainbow spectrum, it lives in the realm of spirit which is neutral.

The seventh chakra is one of unification. To ascend to this point in a chakra practice brings complete bliss aka inner peace. In the original chakra practices used by monks the sole purpose was to connect and stay connected to God.

The culture of the 1960s supported tuning out to tune in, and artists like Janis Joplin, Jim Morrison, and Jimi Hendrix (and too many others to name) used drugs to ascend to the God consciousness that those who used the disciplined process of chakra evolution achieved.

The movement to find what created nirvana naturally led to color healing, and soon the chakras gained momentum. The unconscious became a conscious experience and true feeling of connection.

In the evolution to Westernized culture, it posed the question: *Why am I here?*

The simple truth is that using a relatable path like the law of attraction or manifesting your desires is a large part of chakra magic for many.

However, sustainable bliss must come from a true intention to evolve through our human issues to the highest realm, where we can give back. This is the purpose of grasping the true power of the energies you have inside you.

Ascending to our seventh chakra is not the same as skipping vital steps to achieve the bliss available.

MODERN INTERPRETATION

Much of the material written today describes the chakras; however, the modern interpretation demands that you experience it.

While many people try to work through their issues in the first three chakras, it is challenging to do, as the discipline of the spiritual chakras is necessary to truly create lasting harmony.

We are often staring at our own mythical Trojan horse, as it can be challenging to see what is hidden in a destructive pattern. By using your chakra map, you can begin to use your blocks to build your life rather than stop it.

In many ways the sixth chakra is one of witnessing our wounding and discovering our purpose. The crown chakra is the true ascension to God consciousness—and living out the legacy we came here to fulfill.

This is quite true as we revisit another story regarding hidden agreements, only this time, we witness a purpose emerging from the smoke.

THE LIVING YOUR PURPOSE STORY

A number of years ago when I was working with clients on chakra healing, a prominent healer I knew sent her husband to see me. She was at her wits' end, as he was about to lose his third company. Each time he had built up a company from scratch, made tens of millions of dollars, and in a matter of months run it into the ground.

With children in the home, she had grown weary of losing everything and then watching him rebuild. Through endless fights, therapy, and her own elevated awareness, she finally recognized that it was beyond her capacity in the moment.

So there I was sitting across from Nick, a bright, charming and obviously smart guy, and a great husband. He adored his kids, loved his wife, and if it weren't for this one little thing, everything in their life would be perfect, according to his wife.

While he was mildly interested in figuring things out, he considered his attraction to risk to be a part of success. He also admitted that somewhere inside him he knew he had gone too far whenever he lost everything.

He had been offered $52 million for his company; he held out, saying it was worth more, and the buyers, realizing they were up against no one else, came back with an offer of $36 million.

He was furious, and refused to sell to them.

By the time I met him, that same buyer was about to walk away but had come back with one more offer of $19 million.

Nick was furious: "They're trying to kill me, but I've proved to them that I'll survive."

Looking at this just as an outsider, you would have to say this guy's being an idiot. Even at $19 million it was better than losing everything.

I asked him about that, and he waved his hand in the air, "Aren't you supposed to fix me with your chakra thing or something?"

He was a to-the-point person, so I came out and asked him which one of his grandparents lost everything.

It was his father's father. Since he had been caught off guard by my question, he continued by saying that he "never met the guy, he was one of those people who jumped out of the window during the Great Depression because he lost everything."

"So he was wealthy?"

"Oh yeah, my dad went from living with servants when he was three to having no shoes and living on a dirt farm. My father never recovered."

The hidden agreement that came to me from his sixth chakra was with this grandparent. In order to heal his father, Nick was going to lose everything and prove that he didn't have to kill himself and he would survive.

It was his own choice of words that they were "not going to kill" him that was an indicator of what to look for.

Remember? Our greatest wounding becomes our purpose,
which is often in a hidden agreement in our sixth chakra.

Nick recognized that he was trying to help his father by trying to solve the problem his grandfather had created in the family.

In his case, Nick sold his company for $19 million and began working with people who lost a loved one to suicide. He had found his true purpose by uncovering what he came here to heal.

WHEN YOUR SEVENTH CHAKRA IS UNSETTLED, LOOK TO THE PRIOR ONE

Repetitive patterns can prevent ascension to the seventh crown chakra, which is our personal bliss. Nick's story illustrates what happens when we complete a pattern also known as a "block."

Why, then, not call it a "block"? Remember the use of the word *abandonment* in the third chakra story? When she discovered how she used the word *abandonment*, she was able to recognize that it was not abandonment at all simply by looking at the situation rather than her own feeling.

Do you see how challenges become more easily shifted when we apply them to real life rather than speak in abstracts?

Lingo has its place, certainly. And common language supports us in communicating, but to try to "get over" something can mean ignoring a vital part of who you are.

Chakra evolution is about integrating your life experiences, not cutting them out. All elements are useful in chakra awareness. Each piece of your story is your map, which can create a magnificent tapestry of your journey.

As we move from the idea that we need to "fix our woundings," we can transform them into the fuel that becomes our purpose. This is the true power of the seventh chakra.

THE SEVENTH CHAKRA IS ASCENSION

One does not become enlightened by imagining figures of light but by making the darkness conscious.

—Carl Jung

When we experience the seventh chakra, it is the exhilaration of clear breath. The doors of the seventh chakra open naturally through the pain and emotional challenges we faced in our sixth chakra. When we step into our own dark night of the soul, or the true legacy we've been left, as well as the challenges from our ancestors, and we no longer resent them for being who they were, this is the moment when we light our own Olympic torch.

MEDITATION

A Review of Our Journey / 4–8 Minutes

If you have learned anything about the chakras on our journey together, it was only because you experienced it. One of the telling things about our modern society is that we often dismiss our experiences as perhaps not as valuable unless we have something tangible to show.

Before we begin this meditation, you already know to read this with soft eyes. I am going to remind you that what you have learned intuitively may not translate in this moment to a tangible thing. The ultimate outcome in chakra work is the achievement of inner peace.

Let's begin in the beginning.

Take a breath, bring down the white light, and step into the familiar state of your own internal chakra wisdom that you have journeyed with in this book.

We begin with our root chakra story. Do you remember the story? The two trees: One was given the ice it needed for its own growth. The other was left alone. In this moment, become aware of your own roots: Have they grown? How far have they grown?

Where are they now?

Breathe.

In the second chakra story, there was a woman who was never going to forgive her parents. And although she never did forgive her parents, she discovered she was profoundly loved. The very thing she had focused on was no longer important when her second chakra experienced the emotion of true love. Become aware of your access now to that second chakra within you. Do you remember when we simply called it the color orange? It is now alive within you.

Breathe.

In the third chakra you focused on yellow. The story was of a woman who spent her life having decided that her mother abandoned her. Her third chakra of instinct had driven her into that feeling repeatedly. When we truly stepped into the experience of that feeling, which was felt in her second chakra, her third chakra changed the meaning from abandonment to protection. By simply changing the meaning she had made of a feeling, her entire life changed. In this moment, I invite you to step into your solar plexus, that place of survival, decisions, fight or flight. Can you experience the power here? Imagine what today we call the core is the true harnessing of our earthly thoughts and plans and the direction we will choose for our life.

Take a deep breath as we step into the fourth chakra. The story here was of a girl who wanted a bakery. Do you remember? Do you remember her wanting to recapture the feeling that no longer needed to be held on to? By giving up the dream, she discovered her destiny. This is the true opening of our heart chakra. I invite you to step into that feeling right now and experience the brilliant light that resides in your heart.

Breathe, and we will now step into the fifth chakra. Do you remember the blue light of calm? And in the story, the actress whose hidden agenda was so strong she attracted it directly to her, and instantly. Can you now see the possibility of what can occur when we are not communicating in our highest possible intention in the fifth chakra? Can you also step into the idea here that her goal to be a great actress was met? Because a goal, after all, is who we become in the process of achieving it. She had created an inauthentic situation because that was the communication of who she was. Whether or not she saw this information is not as important as whether you do right now.

Step into your fifth chakra and recognize that we cannot save others from the fate they have created. Breathe.

In the sixth chakra we met Annie. Do you remember Annie? She spent her life seeking love, and she had all the skills necessary. Yet it was a hidden agreement to heal someone that could never be completed until she recognized what the secret was. Once she saw that this pattern had been created by a powerful connection with her grandmother, it shifted. Breathe into this moment and become aware of any feelings you have in your body. As you become aware of this perhaps unsettled feeling, I invite you to recognize that this discomfort is simply part of the process. Do nothing. Just let yourself know that you have everything you need to heal yourself and any inherited agreements. This energy of discomfort can be a very familiar friend when you recognize that this is precisely what the yogis felt as they brought breath and sound into the places that needed it. Go ahead and drop your shoulders; recognize that you are ready for more advanced work with your chakra.

And finally, the story of finding that one's purpose is truly through the door of our wounding. When we look at Nick's story— trying to prove that he could survive losing his fortune when his grandfather couldn't survive—we truly can feel into the idea that the healing, the agreement, was completed. As you take a breath, I'd like to bring your awareness to the idea that once you face your wounding, complete agreements, and really experience your own chakra journey, living your purpose through helping others as you do it is truly the nirvana that we have been graced with in this journey.

APPLYING THE SEVENTH CHAKRA: YOUR MAP HAS YOUR ANSWERS

This is where our Western journey concludes. Yet it does not end, does it? For our purposes we go no further than the seventh chakra in this book. Therefore when you reach the seventh chakra, we begin again with the root chakra, with more awareness than before.

YOUR CHAKRA GROWTH EXERCISE

The Antonym Approach / 3 minutes

Using one of the keywords or phrases from below, write out 3 individual sentences about yourself. The catch is you MUST do this quickly AND write each sentence including one of the keywords or phrases listed below.

Note: You can use a synonym or antonym of a word too—
MAKE IT FUN!

1. Who you were when you began this book.

2. What you discovered about your own chakras.

3. Where you are now in your personal interest in further chakra study.

Keywords and Phrases That Relate to the Seventh Chakra

- **Keywords:** universal, consciousness, truth, communication, loyalty, serenity, faith, spirituality, creativity, expression, purpose, bliss, nirvana

- **Key Phrases:** connecting with spirit, universal ideas, send your intention out to the universe, God consciousness

MANIFESTING INTENTION

This is the God consciousness energy. You are now in the presence of your own ascended consciousness. This is always the outcome.

Seventh Chakra Key Ideas

- You actually experienced, rather than read about your chakras.

- Chakra healing requires the discipline of breathing through challenging feelings.

- As you finish *Chakras*, you discovered you learned more than you thought you did.

- Fears will continually surface, yet how you relate to the issue *is* the issue.

- The connection to your inner God consciousness is alive inside you through your chakras.

- The connection to the past exists in your own lineage—cellular memory is real.

- If we are all connected, then you need only be reminded of your chakras, not taught them.

LOOKING AHEAD

Remember, as we complete the seventh chakra, we return to the first chakra in our wheel. The chakra wheels inside us are always in motion. They remind us that we are never stuck, never lost, and never really blocked. Even when we feel blocked, we have the map as a path to understanding where we are.

LOOKING AHEAD:
CHAKRA RECAP

Let's take a quick spin around the wheel to review where to look on the map and zoom in when discomfort arises in our lives:

FIRST CHAKRA: RED

Beliefs—when you feel that you need to challenge a belief, look here and ask yourself: Did this come from my family of origin?

SECOND CHAKRA: ORANGE

Emotions—when challenging feelings, emotions, or outbursts occur, remember:

If it's hysterical it's historical. Look to the prior chakra to see where the belief came from that created the need for an emotional extreme.

THIRD CHAKRA: YELLOW

Instinct—as we are all wired for survival, when difficult or challenging thoughts are running your life, look back to the emotion that brought it on.

FOURTH CHAKRA: GREEN

Love—as the chakra that divides our physical experiences in life, and our spiritual experiences, the fourth chakra is often the disregarded center of compassion. When you are not accepting yourself, or find yourself in any state that opposes love, look to the heart chakra and apply the filter of love to your circumstances.

FIFTH CHAKRA: BLUE

Communication—anything we send out to the universe—our vibes, our words, our thoughts, our intentions, our deepest desires, and our resentments: all of these expressions are filtered through the fifth chakra. Whether we speak or express nonverbally, we are constantly communicating, and remember: the universe will mirror what we are sending out. Often it will match our energy and send us more of it.

SIXTH CHAKRA: INDIGO

Our sixth sense lives here and holds our visions, intuition, and yes, psychic phenomena. And in this chakra we will notice that painful patterns are directly related to our repetitious communication with the world, whether or not we see it. Looking back at the message we are sending out through the fifth chakra will begin to reveal what perhaps you need to heal.

SEVENTH CHAKRA: VIOLET OR NEUTRAL

As I alluded to, the seventh chakra is a universal consciousness and therefore holds within it the power of the God consciousness and universal agreements. When we look at celebrities or people who are well known to us for one reason or another, we are seeing the universal agreement that something in that person has value to us. To be clear, value does not have to mean we approve of them, remember—because spirit is neutral, it can be that people hate that person, love that person, or don't feel anything but simply know that person. The universal agreement is that people have some kind of response to what is in the universal consciousness.

Your Chakras

As you travel around the wheel here, you've begun to see the pieces of each chakra and how it relates to you. Remember that this is only the opening to the modern chakra concepts and ideas.

The most important takeaway I can leave you with in terms of the chakras is this: Only you can decide if something is true for you, based on whether or not it resonates and works for you.

Your chakra map contains whatever you choose to include on it. What you create and where you go with it can only be decided by you.

CHAKRA CENTERING VERSUS
CHAKRA BALANCING

Notice I didn't say: *balancing your chakras?*

In some ways, the idea of balancing is an advanced concept that asserts that you already know what the chakras are and have experienced your chakras.

I use the word *centering* as a way of making the point that you and your chakras are always in perfect rhythm with your energetic vibration. When we feel off-kilter, disconnected, or unfocused, centering ourselves is a way to get back into personal alignment.

I like to begin with the idea of centering as being invested in your own core. When you meet yourself where you are, then you will always know your own chakras.

For example, a German physician long ago determined that 98.6 was the normal temperature for the human body. Guess what?

Nothing could be further from the truth! While many people do use that as a standard by which to determine when they are off-balance physically, for some the number could be 97.1 or 99.2.

When you look at balancing your chakras without first determining your personal normal, you're measuring yourself against a concept that may not apply to you.

This is why we don't begin with the idea of balance until you have experienced what YOUR chakra center feels like.

THE SOUNDS OF CHAKRAS

If you've ever been to a modern yoga class, chances are you've worked with the concept of controlled breath and vibrational sound. As breath and sound resonate through our bodies, they create a change of state or trance of peace. Each chakra holds old ideas, fears, and our highest energy within it. As we work with sound, we release these chakra endorphins (if you will), creating a place of choice.

CHAKRA SOUNDS: FINDING YOUR VIBRATIONAL CHAKRA PITCH

Let's start with the simple sounds of each chakra as a tool to experience centering. A few ideas to keep in mind:

- Vibrational chakra sound is a tool to calmly experience each chakra.

- Each chakra has a sound that vibrates through vocalization centers and directs peace and centering to that chakra.

- There is no wrong way to do it. If you are confused about the pronunciation of the sound, look online for a sample.

- Chanting aloud directs focus into any chakra when you use

the sound associated with it. This is a way to experience each one.

WHAT IT FEELS LIKE TO BE CENTERED VERSUS NOT CENTERED

Vowels have a melodic tone that vibrates in a frequency that we, in our native language, can understand. This is the best way to describe the experience of being centered in your own chakras. When we are in sync with another person, we are experiencing alignment. Below are a few examples of communication alignment.

Have you ever:

- finished a friend's or loved one's sentence?
- known when someone would call and they did?
- wanted the same food at the same time as a companion?

We call this weird, a coincidence, or cool. Yet it is also an example of what alignment feels like.

When you are *not centered* in your own chakras, it can feel similar to:

- being annoyed for no reason
- feeling like others don't "get you"
- addiction: needing something external to dim an inner disturbance
- being deeply unhappy or lost in your life

Chakra centering is therefore a way of stopping external influence and seeing where you are in any moment, of regaining internal balance as you use YOUR own personal thermostat to define your center. You can then work with more advanced concepts of what balance means to you.

THE SOUND OF CHAKRAS

Before we entertain sound, remember that accents change vowels! Use what we have here as a guideline. Check in your native language for the proper sounds to make. Yes, chakras are a universal language; however, what resonates for you is key, and the way I describe it may make a different sound in your world.

Each chakra has the same resonance as UM. Though it's spelled with AM, imagine saying "UM" with each vowel in front of it.

So LAM is "LUM," VAM is "VUM."

We repeat this chant to allow our body to align with the way sound resonates for you.

- LAM—chakra 1 (root)

- VAM—chakra 2 (sacral/navel)

- RAM—chakra 3 (solar plexus)

- YAM—chakra 4 (heart)

- HAM—chakra 5 (throat)

And we return to the OM that is familiar as we move to the 6th and 7th chakras of higher consciousness.

- OM—chakra 6 (third eye/brow)

- OM—chakra 7 (crown)

As you become more comfortable finding your internal resonance in each chakra, you will naturally find your center. Later,
you can decide if balancing a chakra is something that works
for you.

YOUR MORNING MEDITATION THROUGH YOUR CHAKRA RAINBOW

Tip: Breath is important at the beginning of every meditation. It is used to hold and sustain energy to support us—and is particularly useful when faced with challenging moments.

Begin with a breath; inhale the clean energy surrounding you, hold for 5 seconds, and . . .

Exhale.

As you exhale energetically, imagine releasing anything you don't need into the universe. Like rinsing out a coffee cup; you can do this several times and stop when you feel you have come to center.

This simple meditative visualization is a fun way to do an intuitive daily chakra practice.

The wisdom from your chakras will resonate with one of

these energies, and this will be the energy to work with in the morning as you start your day, or in the evening to wind down, when you will release this energy.

THE MEDITATION

With your eyes open or closed, take a slow deep breath and exhale anything you don't need into the space in front of you. Become aware of a white light energy swirling from the heavens and into the space you are occupying.

As you relax into this light, notice your new internal state— one of being able to see with your mind's eye.

Imagine seven doors in front of you. The first door on your left is red and vibrates with the first chakra.

The door to the right of it is orange and vibrates with the second chakra.

The next door to the right is yellow and vibrates with the third chakra.

The fourth door, directly in front of you at the center, is green and emits fourth chakra energy.

To the right is a blue door, which resonates with the fifth chakra.

The next door to the right is an indigo blue, which calls to your sixth chakra.

And the final door on your right is the seventh chakra, with a violet white light that connects with universal consciousness.

Step back, inhale, and allow yourself to be drawn to the first door that calls to you.

Tip: I recommend that you stay with the first choice that comes forward. The first choice is often your intuition speaking to you; the second choice is your brain second-guessing what your intuitive wisdom is telling you.

Imagine opening the door and stepping into the beautiful light from the chakra that you have chosen. Your choice will awaken your corresponding chakra within, and allow you to connect with the associated spiritual thoughts and tools to use for the day before you.

WHICH CHAKRA DID YOU CHOOSE TODAY?

Did You Pick the First Chakra (Red Door)?

Breathe and experience the power of your roots that support who you are.

Today we will look at the foundation you have chosen for yourself. Are you building on old family beliefs, or are you stretching your roots into a new paradigm of existence? To fully experience your first chakra, let's look at what being in or out of alignment will feel like and observe what the experience is.

Signs of Alignment

- standing your ground
- being willing to grow and consider new ideas
- stepping onto a new platform and offering a hand up

Misaligned

- going against your own ideas
- compromising your integrity
- pretending to want something that you do not
- selling something you don't believe in

Tip: Remembering that what opposes, exposes; any time you feel out of alignment, you can simply create the opposite energy by looking up and choosing an antonym to focus on as you step into the state of that new energy.

Optional Tip: Do 30 seconds of vibrational sound with your chakras to energize your intention for the day.

Did You Pick the Second Chakra (Orange Door)?

If you stepped through the orange door, your second chakra will rule the day. Frequently when our emotions are in charge, they are influenced by the prior foundational energy of the red chakra. Therefore, in order to support and empower your emotional energy, breathe in the orange light, and observe how this energy feels as it vibrates internally.

The orange chakra is a moving, sensuous, and in some ways emotionally demanding energy. The energy can either be contained by the discipline of the second chakra, or it can be unleashed, it and can feel as though you are consistently being disempowered. For the second chakra, alignment is emotional maturity, whereas being misaligned is emotional immaturity.

Emotional Maturity

- listening without reacting; not to be confused with not feeling

- holding compassion for anyone else's inability in the moment to use mature emotional communication

- holding the highest emotional expectation of yourself

- knowing that emotional excellence = being aligned with spirit

Emotional Immaturity

- being energetically judgmental and demanding your way or no way

- being upset with others for not doing something that fulfills you emotionally

- expecting excellence without giving it

- feeling internal pain and screaming at others; having an inability to own upset as a choice

The key to the second chakra today is recognizing when your emotions are running you versus when they are empowering you.

> Tip: If you can step into a state of emotional excellence, and recognize the state, you can at any time turn your emotions around, offering yourself a window into clear thinking.

Did You Pick the Third Chakra (Yellow Door)?

As you step inside the yellow door, you may recognize the warmth of sunshine. Breathe in this soothing God consciousness, and notice the way in which emotional excellence from the prior chakras forms the basis for wise thinking here.

As you move into the power of your third chakra, the ability to quickly process that which is happening in front of you becomes the issue of the day.

Deciding, planning, and stepping into the personal inquiry of *Am I doing what I came here to do?* may become the undercurrent for the day's inquiry.

Yellow chakra thought: Headaches or an inability to think clearly may engulf your present circumstances if you are not in alignment with what you came here to fulfill.

In the third chakra, alignment represents being clear and focused, while being misaligned is confused and unsure. Let's look at some of the things to look for to give you ideas to process the day ahead.

Clear and Focused

- experiencing emotional certainty as you think about your decisions

- knowing the path before you is clear; allowing others to support your plan

- planning out what must be done and having fun doing it

- experiencing questions from others as inquiry rather than inquisition

Confused and Unsure

- making plans or decisions in a highly charged emotional state

- being afraid, and using this emotion in communication with others

- experiencing other people joking as making fun of you

- feeling frustration and quitting over being unable to figure something out

As you can see, the third chakra rests upon the prior chakras of your emotions. Clear thinking and planning stem from the empowered state of emotional excellence.

Did You Pick the Fourth Chakra (Green Door)?

Most often I hear people talk about the heart chakra as the one that needs "balancing." In actuality the fourth chakra is never fully balanced. Remember, a seesaw is meant to go up and down, and there is a natural rhythm to it. A balanced seesaw defeats the purpose of being on one! Today the fourth chakra will reveal your ability to allow circumstances to be as they are without trying to control anything.

The difference is that the ebb and flow of true fourth chakra alignment allows connection to the higher spiritual chakras, versus stagnant energy that prevents our connection with our higher chakras. Alignment is therefore an ebb and flow, whereas misalignment is fearful and alone.

Ebb and Flow

- having a genuine presence, which allows an energetic give and take in a loving manner

- allowing another person the focus and spotlight as you send love to their wins

- experiencing love as coming through you and into the space you occupy and beyond

- reveling in love as your current focus

Fear and Alone

- a personal sense of restriction and inability to join in festivities

- mistaking pity for love and not recognizing that being less-than garners pity

- suffering a true internal frustration and upset as you cannot see how to get what you want

- not being able to see love being offered to you

Did You Pick the Fifth Chakra (Blue Door)?

When you step into the blue light behind the blue door, an awareness of the energy you are sending out, whether verbally, silently, or energetically, becomes the focus of your day.

I often refer to the fifth chakra as the manifesting one, as the throat area represents a window into what we have already created in our lives. Every single thing you will notice today is directly related to the energy or intention you have sent out to the universe to this point.

Therefore, when we look at alignment, it really is accepting responsibility for what we have created in our lives. When we experience misalignment, it stems from a hidden belief that someone else has caused our life to turn out the way it has. So today we'll look at the two energies of responsibility versus benefits of irresponsibility. Yes, benefits. There must be a payoff or you would never do it!

Responsibility

- looking around and knowing that you are responsible for everything manifested in your life

- accepting that the state of your life is completely your responsibility; for example, your single state has been created by you and is not due to a lack of eligible partners

- knowing that every single thing has a particular vibrational frequency that you must step into in order to allow it to occur in your life

- knowing that nothing has been done to you; rather, you have created everything through you

Benefits of Irresponsibility

- living comfortably with the idea that you could do "it" if you really wanted to

- holding others responsible for your outcomes, so you do not have the fear of personal judgment around failure

- not needing to recognize that what you have is not what you want

- keeping the fear of not living your purpose at bay and ignoring the feeling that you came here to do something important that you are not doing

In the fifth chakra, we look at how what has shown up in our life is a reflection of who we are.

Did You Pick the Sixth Chakra (Indigo Door)?

Stepping into the intuitive space of the sixth chakra, you'll notice that the indigo light is unlike any other energy. In our Western chakra system, this is our sixth sense. This will be a day to become aware of whether you are living out your own desires or trying to fulfill the will of someone else to heal them. Hidden agreements and beliefs that may not be ours can surface.

Today is about whether you're shutting down your intuition or being true to the intuitive unknown. It is important to be aware that the intuitive unknown is not necessarily a higher or lower choice. The unknown is the space in which we allow the angels to guide us. This in and of itself is a call to uplift our personal state into the God consciousness, which allows us to ascend to the seventh chakra. When we look at alignment versus misalignment, we are looking at a lower vibrational energy versus a higher vibrational energy.

Higher Vibrational Energy

- holding space for someone else's pain without inheriting a need to fix it

- evolving from wounding to purpose by recognizing that your wounds are the keys to your purpose

- being present with your sadness (and that of others) and experiencing it without it defining you

- honoring another person without judgment and supporting them by validating their life experience

Lower Vibrational Energy

- quoting clichés to fix others and avoiding a true investment in the relationship

- creating a false self, one that has more invested in looking good than in being real—and the two are easily confused

- thinking you have the answer for others, when you have yet to resolve the same issues in your own life

- trying to teach what you don't know while lacking the empathy necessary to open a space for true evolution

As you look through your day, become aware of where you have been and where you will be tomorrow.

> **Tip: If the sixth chakra has called to you, you may want to consider taking one idea a day and focusing on it for eight days. Many of our personal issues will come to a head in the sixth chakra.**

Did You Pick the Seventh Chakra (Violet Door)?

If you have chosen the seventh door, upon opening it you will see a vast expanse of the night sky. Imagine that, in the heavens, a door is opening. Light is pouring down through the stars and into you. Wisdom, universal struggles, and wins—things that affect us all internally and externally—are going to be the essence of your day.

One of the more interesting things about the seventh chakra, aside from it being the only one in our Western system that is not located in our body, is the idea that we are either in alignment with the universe in sharing ourselves and our creative souls, or we are misaligned and trying to take what is not ours rather than occupying a shared reality. Therefore the higher vibrational energy of the seventh chakra is stepping into our personal God consciousness, versus living in our shadow self and fearing that sharing means personal invisibility.

God Consciousness Energy

- knowing that nothing is yours to keep; what comes to you is not owned, but rather shared

- accepting that ultimately you ascend to your highest consciousness, which is beyond ownership of anything

- witnessing how true creative people allow the energy in without censoring the beauty of their personal gift—knowing they are not the gift; they are merely the shepherd for it

- honoring the fragility of other people, knowing that we are all one criticism away from quitting, yet there are those who don't

The Shadow Side

- fears life and experiences universal connections as unsafe

- prevents visibility by living in resistence to the shadow side which keeps them looking peaceful, yet they are not experiencing that on the inside

- places everything on the achievement of one specific outcome—this attempt to control their world shuts down the possibility of something bigger than they can imagine

- avoids sharing our perceived dark side with others, not recognizing that this is what prevents true creativity, connection, and oneness to be achieved

Therefore the seventh chakra invites us to look at the parts we are playing today as we participate in the world. And ask ourselves: How do we contribute or refuse to contribute?

NIGHTTIME RITUAL
FOR CHAKRA HEALING

As you wind down your day, allow yourself to release any awareness that came up. Let go of where you were, where you want to be, and where you think you should be.

Let's return to the seven doors. You are now where you were in the morning, and now we are going to count backward from the seventh chakra.

Imagine your crown chakra sending light to the seventh chakra door as it gently closes for the night.

And breathe.

Now, we move back to our sixth chakra and allow our third eye to connect with the light from that door as it gently closes.

And as we take another breath, we send the energy from our fifth chakra, exhaling through the fifth chakra door; all of the day's issues, connections, and communication are offered up into the universe, releasing us from the day.

We turn to the green door, now slightly ajar, and we once again send gratitude, thanks for the day, and love to anyone in the world who needs blessings as the door gently closes.

The yellow door opens, and our third chakra needs of survival are released into the sun emanating from the doorway. We recognize that our thinking is as it should be as the door gently closes and sends our thoughts and plans back to the universe to cleanse.

The second chakra opens to allow any leftover emotion in our body from the day to be released into the heavens. We can now send any emotions beyond a calm vibration through that second chakra door.

As that door closes, the final red chakra door opens. We offer thanks for all the beliefs that we no longer carry, for all of the wisdom from our ancestors, and for the growth we can now experience through the centering of our own chakras.

The first chakra takes with it anything from the room, from our space—anything that is not peace, anything that is not love—through the first chakra door.

The final door closes as the vacuum seal of the world has been closed for now, to allow us to fully rest for the night.

And so it is.

FINAL THOUGHTS

Keep in mind that ALL of us who teach or study chakras do it through the lens of our own personal experience. You have started a journey and I encourage you to continue to grow and change. I send you blessings on the road ahead, and it is my deepest wish that your path is lit by love.

—Tori

ADDITIONAL RESOURCES

As you can see already, this book has been more about experiencing your chakras than learning about philosophy that does not really apply to how we live today. We are more interested in application than abstract terminology.

Books

There are many books on chakras. This is a very small list; by no means comprehensive:

Rainbow Body: A History of the Western Chakra System from Blavatsky to Brennan, by Kurt Leland, Ibis Press. I LOVED this books. Kurt Leland is perhaps one of the most researched books I have found. That said, it is NOT light reading. However it is excellent and will fill in historical gaps. If you are seeking a comprehensive guide to history, START HERE.

The Serpent Power: The Secrets of Tantric and Shaktic Yoga, by Arthur Avalon, Dover Publications. This book was a very advanced read.

It is believed that since large parts of this book were translated from Sanskrit there is material lost in translation. Arthur Avalon (pen name for Sir John Woodroffe [1865–1936], a respected British Kundalini expert) refers in his book to the six chakra system (in Western we added the third eye color of indigo). This is a challenging book to read, yet it is considered one of the most pure textbooks we know of regarding Kundalini meditative practice and its connection to the chakra system's development.

The Chakras, by C. W. Leadbeater, Quest Books. The author was a clairvoyant as were many of those who developed our understanding of the chakras. It was published in 1927. A well- known text frequently referred to on the road to chakra understanding in the west.

Bodymind, by Ken Dychtwald, Tarcher Putnam. Ken Dychtwald was a part of the human potential movement that integrated the mind-body with chakras. While mind-body later added the word *spirit*, that did not come until much later. For most of the 1970s and the 1980s Dychtwald was one of the leaders of this movement. This book connects the rainbow colors to the chakra, further confirming the first modernized adaptation of the chakra connecting with the rainbow. START HERE to go further into mind-body connections and discover some of the roots of the human potential era.

The Seven Keys to Color Healing: A Complete Outline of the Practice, Roland T. Hunt, Harper Collins. In this book, author Roland T. Hunt connects the use of color to healing ailments. It is wordy and at times hard to wade through, however as he was part of the human potential movement this introduction to the power of color further solidified the connection of the western color choices (rainbow colors) with the chakras.

There are many chakra books, yet the two below I truly feel are excellent and offer a true understanding that will enhance what you have learned in this book:

The Chakra Bible: The Definitive Guide to Working with Chakras, by Patricia Mercier, Sterling. I loved Patricia Mercier's book. There are quite a few ideas here, and her work is genuinely authentic. You cannot go wrong having this book on your shelf.

Chakras Made Easy: Seven Keys to Awakening and Healing the Energy Body, by Anodea Judith, Hay House UK. Agree or disagree, Judith Anodea is the undisputed guru in quite a bit of our westernized chakra work. She indeed has contributed to the evolution of chakras and every book by her has juicy tidbits to take in and consider.

Video

While Gaia has a great selection of chakra videos—most are attributed to yoga. Follow your own map as you look over their selection and choose what calls to you. I only picked one as I am very familiar with Christopher Hareesh Wallis's work:

Tantrik Micro Meditation Practices, by Christopher Hareesh Wallis. Wallis is one of the most brilliant teachers of chakras that I can recommend. Gaia has this stunning video series with him and I HIGHLY recommend it. Go deeper into the chakras AND he will introduce you to the twelve chakras—he himself knows and understands the outer chakras and has studied them for decades.

Music

https://www.soundstrue.com Another great resource to find chakra music, chants, and teachings.

Chakra Suite: Music for Meditation, Healing and Inner Peace by Steven Halpern.

ACKNOWLEDGMENTS

There is nothing more rewarding than thanking people you think the world of in your book acknowledgments. Particulary when they have steered your ship for a long time.

Joel Fotinos. I have known you for more than twenty-five years, yes true, and when you asked if I would join in your first project with St. Martin's Essentials, I was honored. Thank you, Joel, sincerely. What fun!

Monte Farber and Amy Zerner, you have been friends, role models, and support for more than thirty years. You both inspire me, perhaps more than I have ever told you. Now is the time to do so.

My agent, Christopher Wold, whose unwavering faith in me has kept me moving forward no matter what. You are so much

more than an AGENT. An advisor, guide, sharp as a tack nego-
tiator and someone I admire.

My creative sister, SARK, whom I'd admired for many years
and then one day she reached out to tell me she admired MY work,
validated my intuitive journey when I needed it most. Thank you.

Amanda Turner. Wow! You told me to keep going and had
my back on this project! You read pages, assured me that there
was a there in here, and I loved taking on the discipline of a professional writer with your guidance. I appreciate and admire your
talent.

And Sara Murphy, who stepped in as my researcher on the
chakras and gave me valuable notes that formed the direction for
this book. Thank you.

ABOUT THE AUTHOR

Cat Ford-Coates

Tori Hartman is a professional intuitive and author of the best-selling *Chakra Wisdom Oracles Cards*. Following a near-death experience almost twenty years ago, Tori was visited by a spirit who told her a collection of brightly colored stories. These stories prompted her lifelong fascination with color, the chakras, and their power to transform and heal lives. Tori is based in Asheville, North Carolina.